DEDICATION

This book is dedicated to Denis Mullins and the Garda Drugs Squad team; to the drug clinic and all the staff in Jervis Street; to my family, who are wonderful; to Gay Byrne and John Caden; to Dr. Tony Peacock; to my long-suffering editor and everyone at Ward River Press; to the Adelaide Hospital; to James Comberton and Coolemine; to Mary, who has remained a loyal, sincere and true friend and stuck by me since I was nineteen; to all addicts who are seriously trying to come off drugs; to the parents of addicts; to my flatmates and neighbours, with thanks for all their support; and lastly, to myself.

D1556081

AUTHOR'S NOTE

This book is disjointed, mixed up, because I am disjointed and mixed up. There's a lot that I can't remember, as over the years of my drug addiction I suffered such frightful black-outs — loss of memory — that *no* amount of trying to recall certain events will bring them back to my mind.

The book is also full of contradictions, because in writing each chapter I would suddenly remember something that I had completely forgotten, and my mind would become clearer ... and then it would go hazy again about my experiences of the past ten years.

PUBLISHER'S NOTE

The idea of this book came into being, in the first instance, from a radio programme. One year ago, the Gay Byrne show on RTE radio featured a full-length interview with a young Dublin woman, identified only by the pseudonym "Lisa", who had an extraordinary tale to tell.

She had become addicted to drugs while still a schoolgirl, seeking refuge in pills from the emotional problems of growing up. Very quickly, she progressed to harder and more dangerous drugs, in tough and dangerous company. Soon she was caught up in a horrifying world of constant illness, hospitalisation, petty crime, prostitution and even drug pushing to sustain her habit. Like Alice in Wonderland falling down the rabbit-hole, it was as if "Lisa" had fallen through a trapdoor in society's stage, into a hidden world which few of us could recognise or even imagine, although it exists all around us.

Lisa's story was sensational. But she did not tell it in a sensational manner. In fact, she was quiet, soft-spoken and reticent. Only the gentlest, most tactful interviewing drew her story from her, and overcame her hesitation in speaking of her painful and often humiliating experiences during her years as an addict. It was this quiet, unsensational presentation that gave the interview its compelling power. Here was no vicious dope fiend, just a decent, well-meaning girl from a caring family, trapped in the nightmare of drug addiction. This was a story that anyone could relate to, a person that everyone could get to know.

When we spoke to Lisa about the possibility of doing a book about her experiences, she agreed to co-operate. There were two possible ways of producing such a book. One would be to hire a competent journalist or "ghost" writer to listen to her story and then write it up into a readable story. This method is often decried, but it sometimes produces good results in putting across the experiences of famous people who might be good talkers but are incapable of writing an interesting book. The other way, far more risky but potentially more rewarding, would be to have her set down her own story in her own words.

Writing a book can be a gruelling experience, even for somebody in the best of health. For a young woman exhausted by her continuing struggle against drug addiction, the challenge was even more daunting. But Lisa was a determined character, a fighter and a born survivor. She was perfectly willing to tackle the writing herself, however painful and harrowing some of it might be. And the notebook which she had prepared before the RTE interview showed that she had real writing talent, a vivid personal style, an energy and urgency all her own.

So, for many months and many meetings, she filled notebook after notebook with laborious handwriting. The story she told did not emerge in strict sequence; rather, it was a series of short variations on the main themes in her life — her personal feelings, her experiences of hospital, her friends, her drugs. Sometimes there were gaps or jumps in the story. Sometimes she repeated herself, or returned to the same topic from a different point of view. The editing of the manuscript therefore involved a certain amount of cutting and rearranging of material, so as to make it intelligible to the reader, and the publishers are particularly grateful to Íde Ní Laoghaire and Iris Buchanan for their help in producing a manageable copy-edited typescript of the book. No attempt was made, however, to bridge the gaps, to bring in outside writers, to offer explanatory comments or excuses, or to put opposing points of view. This is Lisa's own book.

Some readers, inevitably, will feel that this approach stays too much inside the author's personal viewpoint, that it fails to appreciate the views of others, and the honest efforts made by so many people — family, friends, teachers, doctors, social workers, Guards — who have found themselves in charge of Lisa. And indeed, she can be harshly critical of people who wielded power over her. Sometimes, she may be downright unfair. But this book is her own view of the world, seen from within the isolated viewpoint of drug addiction. Although one could argue that this is a distorted view, it might be far more helpful to accept her experience and try to learn from it. (Some names and locations have, however, been changed or concealed, in order to avoid causing needless offence, while the author's anonymity is preserved so as to minimise distress and embarrassment to herself and her family).

In the long run, Lisa is hardest on herself. She portrays her own weaknesses far more ruthlessly than she exposes the shortcomings of others. Her book is not a tract on the evils of drugtaking or the failings of public health administration. It is a heartfelt record of the hopes and fears, the triumphs and failures, the good times and the bad times of one young woman.

CONTENTS

LISA

Chapter 1

Schooldays

Your schooldays are supposed to be the happiest days of your life. But my memories of school are all bad.

School — oh man! It started with my first primary school. There's always one picked on in the class, and unfortunately it happened to be me. I didn't live in a "nice" house. We didn't have as much money as other girls' parents. I was never allowed to forget that.

I was always a very sensitive, "difficult" child but that school turned me into a nervous wreck, a trembling mass of nerves. I developed a stammer. I started wetting the bed every night.

I had no friends — I heard the other pupils saying that I wasn't fit to mix with them, that I was dirty, (I was *never* dirty), that my parents couldn't afford a proper house. In the playground, children used to form a ring around me and chant: "Lisa is a knacker, Lisa is a knacker! Lisa lives in a smelly old dump! Lisa can't read or write!"

I was so nervous of the nuns that I was unable to learn anything. I had withdrawn so much into myself that half the time I didn't hear what the teachers were saying. So I was labelled backward and retarded. Once, they pinned a piece of cardboard to my jumper with those words written on it. I was seven years old.

I was unable to do my lessons, unable to produce homework, unable to answer questions — unable to read, write or spell. Because of this I was beaten and kicked and pinched, had my hair pulled; I was put in a cupboard that was called "the hole", and locked in there for hours on end. Have you *any* idea what it was like to be locked into a cupboard? A dark, damp cupboard smelling of disinfectant. No windows, just blackness, blackness, blackness. The unspeakable terror! Will they forget about me? Oh, please, God, let me out. I promise to be good. Good? Good? Jesus Christ, I wasn't bad, was I?

I never told my parents what was going on. The nuns threatened to write to my parents to say I was misbehaving, causing trouble in class and refusing to do my lessons. They said they would send a report home about my disgraceful conduct and that my father would spank me.

I could never finish the Our Father or the alphabet, and the nun who taught religion used to beat me.

One day in another class I got stuck trying to answer a question. I remember being taken down to the toilets, where the teacher interfered with me sexually. I knew something "bad" and "nasty" and "dirty" was happening to me, but it was not until years later that I realised I had been assaulted. For years after that episode, I used to cringe every time my mother kissed or hugged me — I could not bear any woman touching me.

Another punishment that I remember — I'm sorry all my schoolday memories are so bad, there *must* have been good times as well — was when I was in the school chapel for hours on end, praying "for the devil to leave me". According to the nuns, I had the devil in me and would never go to heaven. But I think the most humiliating experience of all was having my hair fine-combed, then washed in a foul-smelling lotion — "for lice" — in front of the whole class! I *never* had lice. Never.

As I had no friends, I began to invent friends. I even invented a dog. I couldn't wait for school to end so that I could play with and talk to my "friends". I loved to bring my "dog" for walks, pour all my love out to him, pretend he was sleeping at the end of my bed — I *loved* that "dog", and I loved my imaginary friends. I was still very young.

When I was about ten or eleven, my father got a new job and decided that he would send us on to a fairly exclusive school — uniform, the lot. Oh, God, I thought the first school was bad; this one was worse. "The school for the élite", that's what we were told. I was put in a class with pupils three or four years younger than me as I still was unable to read, write or spell properly. I was jeered at and teased unmercifully by both pupils and teachers.

After a couple of months, I started breaking out in spots and they were very bad. I was put in a desk away from the rest of the pupils in case they would "catch something" from me. The nuns used to make cruel remarks such as "Are they contagious?" "We don't want the rest of the class catching anything unpleasant."

I wasn't able to tell the time or read the clock. It wasn't really that I *couldn't*, but I used to get a sort of mental block when they asked me to read the time. The school clock was at the bottom of the stairs. The senior pupils were upstairs, juniors downstairs. When the nuns realised I was unable to read the time, although I was nearly twelve years old, they made sure that everybody knew about it. I had to stand under the clock. The jeering I received from *all* the school! Infants to seniors. Another bad memory.

I was *never* invited to parties or outings. I still had no real friends. I suppose I was a difficult, awkward kid, but the isolation was cruel. The *hurt*, the emotional hurt those nuns and my "classmates" put me through. The nights I cried myself to sleep because of the deep painful hurt inside me; the loneliness, the shame, the fear. Even though I had only imaginary friends, I now had a real dog. He took the place of friends and of my parents — he was someone I could pour out all my unhappiness and loneliness to. He was everything to me. And he loved me too. I could not wait for school to finish each day because I had him to come home to.

* * *

I was about twelve years old when a great change came over me. I was growing up, I was changing fast, and I knew, somehow, that I wasn't going to go on like a frightened child forever. Somehow, I summoned up all my determination and decided I'd simply had enough. No more was I going to tremble in fear of those nuns and classmates! No way was I going to allow myself to be the scapegoat, the baby, the joke of the school. I would endure no more mental torture. I had had it and for good! I had changed inside. Look out school, here I come — and with a bang! A personality so changed, so charged with anger — red hot anger — that I gave more trouble than any other pupil ever in the entire school. Unlike James Dean, I was a rebel *with* a cause. I wanted to shock that school. I would make them take notice.

At first it all seemed very positive. I started conforming, started trying to live up to their expectations. Once I made the effort, I found that I was pretty good at gym, tennis and basketball. So I was put into the gym displays, the class tennis team, the basketball team. This "improvement" amazed the teachers! (Teachers? They never even tried to teach me. They never *bothered* about me. I was put down as a dunce from the day I walked into that school because of reports from the previous school. I was in a school for the élite, and I was just a nobody from a common family with a father working himself to the bone to give me a good home and a good education — all the things I had been deprived of for so long; a house to bring friends — what friends? — home to; comfort for my mother — all the things we never had).

Next, it was discovered that I could actually sing. Halleluja! Put her in the school choir! And finally, like the awakening dawn — it was just unfortunate it took so long to awaken — it was discovered that I had some talent at debating. I could talk away on a given subject, logically and coherently, with a command of English that astounded me even more than it amazed my teachers. So I was let into the debating society of the school. I could see them all looking at me in surprise and saying "where has she *been* all these years?" But through it all I was planning trouble. Trouble with a capital T! They didn't know what was about to hit them.

Everything was plain sailing for the first six months or so. Our teams did brilliantly at sports. The choir sang beautifully at the school mass. And I was one of the good girls now. One of the élite.

But all the time, throughout all this newfound "popularity", I had not forgotten or forgiven my earlier humiliations. I was just biding my time. I was going to let all hell break loose; to cause as much trouble and destruction as possible.

I started in little ways. One day, when the nuns were at prayers, I bolted the door of the chapel. Another day, I set off the fire-alarm, and caused panic throughout the school. I found a tin of paint one evening — a disgusting shade of pink — and splashed it over the tennis court.

Another time I sneaked into the gymnasium and arranged an extremely artistic, intricate display of garments from the laundry-basket, looped across the bars, the climbing ropes and the climbing frames. It looked terrific! Like Christmas. Next morning there was nothing to be seen of my artistic efforts, but there were lots of red faces.

One morning I was followed to school by dogs. I was late that day. As I came into the school, I began to run. I rushed into the building, dogs tearing after me, and ran around the school corridors shouting: "Oh, sister, sister, help, there's four dogs chasing me! Oh, sister, miss, *HELP!*" Classroom doors opening, girls joining in the chase, followed closely by nuns. The noise! Pupils screaming, other pupils shouting out advice on how to corner the dogs, me shouting "HELP, HELP!" Dogs barking, nuns' veils flying like sails on a boat. Reached my classroom, burst into the room, dogs after me. The nun jumped on to her desk calling on all the saints there ever were to help her. Help *her!* What about *me,* being chased by four mad (ahem) dogs! Some of the girls shot out the door and ran smack into the nuns and girls tearing up the corridor. Talk about the Charge of the Light Brigade! Eventually, all was quiet on the western front. Some of the girls brought the dogs out, and closed the school gates so there would be no danger of their getting in again. Of course, the school was in uproar. I got three cups of hot sweet tea to calm me down! (I *never* liked tea).

* * *

Even though I was doing better at sports and debating, my academic work was still frightful, so the nuns sent me to be assessed by a psychologist in a Child Guidance Clinic. For two hours I tried to put coloured blocks together into a shape that I had to copy from a sheet of shapes I was given. Finally, the psychologist shot up off his chair, swept the blocks off the table on to the floor in a grand gesture — *very* controlled temper — and said through clenched teeth: *"Get your mother in here!"* I never saw him again.

Around this time I became friendly with a girl from overseas who came to the school, and with another girl whose parents owned a chemist shop. "Naomi", "Janet" and I were more or less three misfits. One day, after basketball practice, I went into the school showers and saw Naomi and Janet with a pile of coloured pills. Naturally, I asked what they were doing, but I didn't get the answer one might expect today: "Here, take some, they will make you feel really happy." Oh no, what I got was: "Open your mouth to *anyone* and we will flatten you!" It wasn't until a week after this episode that I was offered one, then two, then three pills, then any amount I wanted. Those girls were always loaded with pills.

It was about this same time that I had started eating huge amounts of Codeine and Veganin. Well, those pills did it for me. I felt peculiar, but happy and uninhibited. I was twelve-and-a-half. From then on, I openly gave the school trouble. I didn't care! I was so unhappy at school and things seemed to be changing at home. I gave that school hell and felt *no* remorse. I still don't.

At the semi-finals of the debating tournament, I made the silliest speech that anyone had ever heard. Totally incoherent. We lost. Knocked out of the finals. Naturally, I wasn't very popular with my team after that. The nuns were confused, and, I think, a little suspicious.

By now I had become openly defiant in class; aggressive, rude, cheeky, with a couldn't-care-less attitude. The tablets the girls were giving me contributed to a lot of my outrageous conduct — but something else had also broken inside. It was a combination of the two. I disrupted classes. I told the nuns to go to hell and stay there when they criticised my schoolwork. Our maths teacher spent a whole class explaining something in geometry to us. But when it came to my turn to answer questions, I hadn't a clue. The whole thing was double Dutch to me, and I told her so. She was obviously at the end of her tether, and I got a slap across the face. "You stinking, frustrated old cow!" I shouted at her. Naturally I was sent to the head nun, who gave me a boring lecture on my behaviour and a letter for my parents, which I tore up as soon as I got out of school — after reading it first. I was suspended for four days. For some reason, I burst into tears when I read that.

In spite of my bad schoolwork, the nuns were still singing my praises for basketball. But within a matter of weeks, the songs of praise had turned to howls of rage and fury. I was the cause of losing a match for the school in a basketball tournament, by deliberately passing the ball to the opposing team. The two sides were level, and I had been in a position to score. They raced down the court and scored the winning point while my team watched, dumbfounded.

I had become very uninhibited. I openly and defiantly caused trouble, and I became wilder and completely uncontrollable. The little coloured pills that my two schoolfriends shared with me helped me to change. They brought me a kind of false happiness. But deep down, I was still very unhappy.

Chapter 2

On the Scene

One of the letters which the nuns sent home to my folks suggested that I should be sent to a school for wayward, uncontrollable girls somewhere down the country. By a coincidence, my father had threatened me with the same thing a few weeks previously. My behaviour at home was getting as bad as that in school — if not worse. In fact, I was getting quite impossible to live with.

When the summer holidays were up, yours truly didn't return to school. Expelled! Kicked out! "Very disturbed child," "one of the most badly behaved pupils we have *ever* had." "What got into her?"

Bloody hypocrites! You never told my parents what you put me through for years. The jeering, the humiliation, the hurt, fear, anguish. No, you didn't tell them that, Sisters!

Freedom! Praise the lord! Shame? I felt no shame, just a tremendous sense of relief. No, the shame wasn't mine, the shame was the school's, the establishment's. The status quo. Oh, blessed freedom. Liberty. Now, I was able to hang out in Stephen's Green. Not just at weekends, but every day, all day. Reality had, at this stage ceased to exist. My two "friends" had introduced me to friends of theirs who were junkies while I was still at school.

* * *

What I hadn't known was that the sister of one of my two girl-friends was a hard drug addict, and was also into pushing heavy gear in a pretty big way.

For about three weeks, I used to get barbiturates from the two girls for nothing. Then, one day, Naomi asked me could I manage to get her ten pounds, as she had lost a ten-pound note her mother had given her to get messages. She told me she'd give me a few extra barbs if I could get her the money. That night, I stole money for the first time in my life — and was to continue stealing for many years to come.

A few days later, she asked me for money again, this time telling me straight out that as long as I gave her cash she would never see me short of barbs. The following month, Naomi, Janet and I went into town one Saturday. We went up to Stephen's Green and my two "friends" introduced me to a load of guys and girls, most of them obviously smashed out of their heads, and all aged something between sixteen and twenty-four years of age. One of them was Naomi's sister.

Then two of the guys, and Naomi and her sister, brought me to a flat not far from the Green. There were a couple of men, one woman and five other teenagers there. I remember one of the men asking Naomi's sister, "has she started fixing yet?" — I didn't even know what "fixing" meant. One boy went out for a few minutes, came back with a syringe, and in front of everybody rolled up his sleeve and plunged the syringe into his arm. I was already feeling mesmerised by the weird, mad flat and the even weirder people, but you can imagine what I felt when I saw *that* happen! Later, one of the girls stuck the same syringe into her leg. That girl was to become, within two years, one of my very closest "junkie" friends.

I was feeling very nervous, and particularly worried by the man and woman who seemed to be in charge of everything — they also seemed to me to be in charge of all the guys and girls who were there. They kept talking in whispers to Naomi's sister, and every now and then they looked over at me, peering at me intently, as if sussing me out. Then the woman came over to me, and without saying a single word she got two pills out of her pocket and handed them to me. Behind her, the man whispered: "you'll get a better buzz out of these than you ever got from barbs."

That was my first introduction to "speed" —

amphetamines. Although I really only wanted to stay on barbiturates, I swallowed the two pills that I had been given, and in a very short time I began to feel as if I had taken flight — actually grown wings. Oh, man, did I speed! The only trouble was that I didn't stop until the middle of that night. I was scared — really very frightened.

The next day, back at school (this all happened before they expelled me), I told Naomi that I just wanted barbs in future, and I asked her what the hell kind of place that was that she had taken me to. Why hadn't she told me her sister was into hard drugs? "Naomi, that crowd in the flat, they were drug addicts, the guys and girls were, anyway." Naomi said nothing, just smiled, and then she asked me casually, "did you enjoy the feeling from those pills?"

I told her I had, but I was very frightened afterwards.

"Believe me, Lisa, you won't feel a bit scared after taking them a few more times."

"I'm not taking those things again!"

"Look, pet, they just take a bit of getting used to, that's all. They'll do far more for you than your barbs. You'll want nothing else once you get used to them. Honest!"

Oh, fool — naive, childish fool — impressionable, foolish child! Naomi asked me had I the bread for the barbs. Yes, I had. Stolen from my family. Then, I noticed for the first time a subtle change in her method. Before that day, she'd hand over the barbs and I'd give her the money afterwards. Or she'd even wait a couple of days for the money if I hadn't got it, letting me have the pills anyway. But this time, I had to hand over the cash first. And the price she was asking for the next supply had gone up. Not much — just from ten pounds to thirteen pounds. Thirteen pounds or no barbs.

"By the way, Janet and me are going back to the flat next Saturday. Like to come along? Feel good?"

I didn't refuse, although I was getting more than a little frightened of her by now. The brutal fact is, I needed those barbs, so I would have stood on my head for Naomi, would have followed her to the ends of the earth — anything, anywhere! If I had had any idea, if I could have seen into the future, I would have known that I was going to depend on that woman and those two men for my "lifeline" for many a year to come. If only I had known ...

Chapter 3

From My Diary

A fantasy: I walk into a field. The grass is wild and uncared for — it's more like a wilderness than a field. In the distance I can see mountains. They are outlined against the sky very clearly. They are very jagged. I come to a wood. It's very dense. Dark. Thousands of old oak trees and a lot of paths. I could easily get lost, but I don't think I'd mind. I'm lost anyway! I come to the sea. There is a sea-chest half buried in the water. I wade in. It's very difficult to open, but I keep at it until, eventually, I manage to open it. It's full of books. Full of knowledge. I start crying with frustration 'cause I don't know which book to start on. I see someone on the beach. Male. I'm frightened by this person. The closer I get to him, the further he goes away. I keep on running after him. Finally he stops moving away from me. I *still* can't see his features, but there's a beautiful aura emanating from him and I'm no longer afraid. We walk into the sea. I could go *anywhere* with this person.

Oh God, help me. Help me to understand myself. I don't like those two girls, only their little coloured capsules. Help me God, damn you, help me! No, don't bother, I don't want to live. Live in this jungle? This mass of confusion? All I want to be is happy. Even with those capsules I'm not happy — oh, yeah, I'm more or less outside of reality — but I still hurt and hurt badly inside.

Sometimes I feel I'm just a voice crying out in the wilderness. I know people hear me — but do they really hear me, does my desperation get beyond their ears? I'm afraid to shout for help, for fear of rejection and lack of understanding. Maybe I should scream "Help me" instead of "Please, somebody help and understand and love me". Oh, I don't know. I hate school! I hate home! I hate people! I hate myself! I hate, hate, hate, hate!

I feel I am a tree, but I have no roots. Now I am a tree stump. The odd thing is — I'm shaped like a foetus and I am comfortable. No, I want to be a tree again — but I want roots! I'm no longer a tree stump — just a foetus and I'm no longer comfortable. I feel insecure. I am a river now. Don't know where I'm coming from. I'm very clear. Clear and fresh. I'm flowing very fast now. I'm no longer a river — just a whirlpool. Now I see the tree stump shaped like a foetus again. Now it's in me. I'm a whirlpool with a foetus in me. I'm fighting it! I'm a cabin now. My folks built me out of different pieces of wood, some strong and well put together. The rest is drift wood and is beginning to decay. Jesus, I'm a mess inside.

People come into me a lot, but they only use me when it's raining and cold, or for shacking up for a few nights. Yeah, they only use me. They don't take an interest in me. I'm just a handy old cabin. I like it when people come in, I feel warm and cheerful and — yes — full. But what a mess they leave me in afterwards. My parents never come in, and *they* built me! At the back there is a very dense forest, but there's always this light shining somewhere among the trees — don't know exactly where, though, and that's making me sad and frustrated.

At home, sometimes, I feel I'm looking in through a window at a happy, united family. A mother, a father and sisters — and I cry out inside: "please include me, I belong also." I feel like an alien being. In a sort of "no man's land". Then I hate them and I don't want to belong to that unity. Pop more pills. Take away the desperation, unhappiness, fear. The awful lack of self-confidence. So, I'm branded "bold," "troublesome," "wayward" and so on. Might as well live up to those labels. But I'm not like that! I'm a messed up, unhappy, frightened child! I'm full of contradictions. Disturbed! "Worst pupil the school ever had." And such a disappointment! "We had become so proud of her." And, you, Sister Agatha, your face going like an overcooked turkey, becoming tongue-tied when Dad asked "Why should she behave like that? We knew she had problems. Why were they so bad?"

Chapter 4

Saint Brendan's, Grangegorman

When I went on the Dublin street scene at thirteen, I thought I was the greatest. Only a kid, and mixing with the real way-out grown-up set. A real junior hippie, with the funky Stephen's Green image. We used to love hanging around the Green, stoned, laughing at the "straights", having nothing to do with those ordinary, boring people. Look at me, I'm a freaked-out junkie! Oh yeah, the big image, the real stoned image. Ragged jeans, tousled hair, flowers, love and peace. The raggier the clothes, the better. Going to all-night parties — spaced out, of course.

But as my dependence on the pills increased, the junior junkie scene began to lose its appeal. My parents, seeing me deeply disturbed, started looking for serious professional help.

After doing the rounds of the upper class

psychiatrists, who mostly talked as if they had a hot, hard-boiled egg stuck in their throats, I eventually became a patient in the Mater, having daily half-hour sessions with my very own personal psychiatrist.

Psychiatrist? Good God! Our sessions consisted of one-sided communication, the communication coming from me. He sat behind his desk smoking his pipe, while I sat on the other side inwardly "going up in smoke". In desperation, I talked of the most ludicrous things. I even invented problems — anything to break the unnerving silence, anything to see some sort of expression on his dead-pan face. Enlightenment? Anger? Delight? Humour? No, nothing, except intense concentration as he went through his ritual of stuffing, filling, lighting and puffing his pipe (no doubt of peace!). It was, literally a staring match. I left that office each time a quivering, shaking mass of nerves, of anger and bewilderment. My parents, too, when they came to talk to him, used to leave his office limp and totally frustrated.

I spent nine weeks in the Mater hospital. I was on a lot of sedative tablets, but when a new patient, Susan, was admitted to my ward, I no longer needed the sedation. Oh, I took pills allright, but the "sedation" I received from the new admission was, well, something else — and very familiar! She was in for depression and drug abuse. Her sister was a hardened junkie and kept Susan and me well supplied with tablets. In return we got as many syringes and spikes for her as possible, and kept our mouths shut. This went on for four weeks.

My psychiatrist didn't notice any drastic change in me. He probably thought my drowsiness was due to the sedation. What he thought my elation was due to, God knows. So I spent nine weeks — nine Goddamn useless, non-constructive, non-helpful weeks — in that hospital. Then I was discharged. Cured! Of what? After two weeks at home (still on medication) I began to feel the effects of withdrawals from the "happy pills", and I was still very disturbed. So I had to go back to the psychiatrist.

He admitted me to a private nursing home. I saw him twice a week. No change in him. No change in me. No treatment — just a lot of medication, walks in the garden, table-tennis, lawn tennis, surface talks with the staff, a beautiful bedroom: all at a beautiful price. For what? Discharged, once again. Cured. Cured? I immediately got in touch with my two classmates and their junkie friends and got straight back into my little blue, yellow and purple happy pills — this time at a price. The price wasn't money. I knew somebody who looked after a clinic and I was able to get into the place. All I had to do was supply my classmates with needles and syringes from the clinic. That was the price I paid. So, what did *I* care?

I was only fourteen years of age when all of this happened. I spent two months in a haze of drugs, not to mention a haze of disturbance which was not entirely related to drug abuse. My whole world fell apart. My beloved grandad died and my dog was killed a week later. Emotionally, that dog represented my parents and friends to me, and when he was killed, a part of me died too. I was taken back into the Mater for four days, heavily sedated. Then I was informed that I was going to a nice hospital: St. Brendan's.

* * *

I had never heard of St. Brendan's. Grangegorman, yes, but not Brendan's. I'd be happy there, well looked after — so I was told. The day I left the Mater I was very heavily sedated, so I saw none of the prehistoric buildings in Brendan's, just a clean, very modern unit where I was to be a patient.

My poor parents! They, in their innocence, were "guided" by my psychiatrist. What anguish, what heartbreak they must have gone through.

The patients in Brendan's looked normal and behaved perfectly normally. If they hadn't, I would have blown my mind. I knew I was in a psychiatric unit — I was yet to find out that it was inside Grangegorman. I shall never forget the horror and bewilderment I experienced when, after a week in bed, I was brought for a walk by one of the nurses, and I saw the rest of the hospital. Big, grey buildings. Bars on the windows. Shouting from within. Distorted faces peering out from behind the windows. What was this place? Where was I? No information from the nurse, just evasiveness. A few days later I was informed by one of the patients that I was in Grangegorman. Naturally, I didn't believe her. "This is St. Brendan's, isn't it?" "It's not, it's Grangegorman." One of the nurses had to intervene, as we were on the verge of a free-for-all. She tried to soothe me: "No, Lisa, this unit is St. Brendan's, the rest of the hospital is Grange-gorman." Ha! I soon grew wise. The whole hospital, my unit included, was Grangegorman. St. Brendan's was just a fancy name given to the hospital to try and take away the stigma of the "Gorman". The nut-house. The loony-bin. The mad-house. The mental home.

Except for the one unit, the place looked like something out of the nineteenth century, like a poorhouse. But four "good things" came out of my stay there.

I met three junkies in the unit and then, to my delight, my friend Susan was admitted three weeks after me. Oh, wow, manna from Heaven! Three junkies in my unit! And my new friend Susan from the Mater! Naturally, the five of us hung around together, sinking deeper and deeper, although we hardly knew it, into the living hell of drug addiction, not to mention the living hell of Brendan's, "House of the living dead". The incredible thing was that the five of us were in for drugs and emotional disturbance, yet we could come and go whenever we wanted. We weren't committed to a closed ward. So, while I was still a patient in Brendan's, I was introduced to the Godfathers of the Dublin drug racket. I was also introduced to different, harder, drugs.

At this time too, I first discovered the high price of drugs. So the shoplifting began — clothes, small antiques, jewellery. On our "free time" out of the hospital, we would go into Dublin and sneak these items out of city-centre shops. We'd sell them to a contact, get half the price of what the items cost, then go to the dealer and score whatever drug or drugs we were into. I was into barbiturates and speed at the time. It was very easy to rob barbs in the hospital, or to bribe patients who were on them for sleep. In fact, it was a cinch getting drugs like barbs and amphetamines there, and as for needles and syringes ... but we still went to the middle men on the streets as well.

Looking back at my time in St. Brendan's for drug abuse and emotional disturbance, I feel sick. Sick to think that on both occasions in that hospital I was rarely off drugs. Sick to think that my "disturbance" could have been treated if only someone had sat and listened, given constructive advice, had seen me as an outpatient, had seen me as an adolescent with serious adolescent problems.

Some hallucinatory memories, not necessarily related to my addiction, come from my time in Brendan's. I grew very friendly with an elderly man who had cancer and died there. I was very cut up over his death and pleaded with two of the staff to let me have a look at him in the morgue. They brought me down, showed me into the morgue, and then locked the door after me, as a "joke." Some joke. Locked into a morgue, with dead people wearing brown habits, faces like wax. They had meant to open the door in a few seconds, but a patient in the men's section of our unit became violent and every available person was called on. When they heard the alarm bell, they completely forgot about me and raced back to the unit. When the commotion had died down, my two friends went off to the canteen, then back on duty, and only then did they remember me. When they went to get me out, I am told that I was huddled up in a corner unable to walk or speak.

Chapter 5

From My Diary

I am a boat. A boat in a desert. I go fast — faster — faster. Drifting now. Sinking — surfacing — sinking — surfacing — why can't I stay under? I don't want to surface. I'm beginning to come apart. Bit by bit until I am no longer a safe little boat — just me. Me, with my wicked mind for all to see. Me, exposed to a jungle of hostility, dislike. Me, exposed to life. Well, listen to me, Life. I don't want you. I don't want what you have to offer. I don't like you. Only when you are a haze, then, and only then, can I accept you — when you are far, far away, and I'm in another world, only then can I take you. Life! You pitiful creature. No, not life, me! Oh, Jesus Christ, my head.

Animals always understand, but people don't. I'm tired of having to explain myself. Tired of being misunderstood — tired of misunderstanding.

Dear God,
    Will you give me a break from the hassles in my mind? Just for a few days. Look, man, I need one.

                              Thanks.

I know the day is happy or gloomy just by looking at it through the window. It doesn't shout to tell me.
Question: Why, then, do people shout?
Note to myself: Answer this question. It is important for communicational purposes.
Answer: Maybe I listen more to the day than I do to people speaking.

Be still and let me feel how fascinating the silence is.

I'm putting in the next part of this diary because it was what I felt at the time. I don't want to hurt my parents, and what I wrote is very unfair to both of them. I was the cause of the tension in the family. Life is very hard for the parents of a drug addict.

I hate you Daddy. I hate your voice. Full of aggression, of tension, of anger. I hate and fear you — yet I love you — but you don't love me anymore. Your tension is clotting inside me. So is your aggression. I don't want to be like you, but it seems I'm becoming a carbon copy of your bad points. You hurt people. You hurt me badly. You hurt my sisters, my mother. That voice! Jesus, shut up, shut up or I'll kill you. I will. I will. I HATE you.

I hate you mammy — stick up for yourself, can't you — how can you love that man like you used to? How can you? Bloody bitch — how do you think I feel, seeing you cry because of him. In God's name, tell him to stop shouting. Nothing is his fault, is it? It's all your fault. God, how can you accept that — what are you? How can you keep on accepting, taking the blame when he mislays things? Why don't you shout back at him?

I'm torn in two over both of you. I hate you, Daddy, for your hurtfulness, your shouting, your sarcasm; yet, I love you. And I hate you Mammy for your apparent willingness to let him hurt you, use you. I want to protect you, but you're my mother not my daughter. Why should I become a mental wreck trying to protect you from him? I want a mother. A block of security. A strong tree to lean on — Jesus, why do you let him hurt *me* so much? Why do I get told off when I justifiably try to defend myself against him — also when I try to defend you? I'm shouted at. I'm sick of being shouted at. Oh, God, fight back. It's like watching a tennis match with one player aceing the ball and the other player feebly returning it and *never* getting it over the net.

Look, I love you both — oh, how I love you — but you're tearing me apart, killing my love for you. You say that I'm killing your love for me with

41

my behaviour, my personality change. But you're doing it too. And you're adults! I wish you could read this — no, I don't. They're *my* feelings; it's *my* diary and like the deep hurt inside me, it's *never* going to be exposed. It's going to stay locked and hidden and I'm going to stay locked and hidden too. Hey, in case you don't know — I am a person — despite what I have been taught about myself in school!

I want so much to learn new things. If only I could read as fast as my mind wants. First I have to learn to see. Some things make me happy and other things make me want to be happy. I always seem to be fighting myself.

It's very quiet and I feel lonely and sad. I can't stop crying. I think my dog can feel my unhappiness 'cause I feel a sort of understanding from him. A comfort. Just holding him tight. Loving him. Being loved by him. Empathy.

My prayer as a child:
> Dear God,
>
> I'm scared and I need someone to lean on. Watch over me. Guide me. Make me happy.
>
> Amen.

My prayer as a young teenager:
> Dear God,
>
> I remain that child.
>
> Amen.

In becoming part of someone else, you lose part of yourself because you are giving of yourself, but the part you lose doesn't matter because in losing it you gain something very rich, rewarding and fulfilling — wow, that's confusing but I know what I'm trying to say, do you?

Oh, help me, somebody; please help. My mind and body feel weird. Oh, God, I'm sick, I think. Maybe I'm taking too many Veganin and Codeine. Oh, Jesus Christ, I feel desperate — maybe I'm going to die. Do I want to die? I mean, really want to? I honestly don't know — all I know is that at this moment in time I feel so sick I don't care whether I live or die.

Fourteen, forty-two, fifty-five, twenty-three, three, fifty — all ages in a row — forced to stay — maybe enjoying it — everybody being forced to forget about their going and to do as much as possible with waiting.

One of the reasons I'm giving so much trouble at home, and this is different from school, is because I feel unwanted and in the way, and this is *my* way of calling attention to myself, to let people know I'm a person with fears and failings, hopes and ambitions — I have feelings. I want to sort of tell people: "Look, listen, I'm Lisa, please let me know that you know I'm around. Please want me. Please help me to understand myself, 'cause I don't know what's wrong with me and I want help. It's not 'cause I'm taking tablets, even without them I still feel — oh, I don't know — all mixed up and so

unhappy and confused. I feel like a see-saw, a
swing, a chairoplane — my mind feels that way.
God, I feel I'm just groping blindly in the dark to
call attention to my unhappiness, my desperate
need for love, my need to be cared about, my need
to be cared for, my *scream*, my silent scream, for
help and understanding."

Why don't I turn that silent scream into a verbal
plea? Fear of rejection, that's why. Fear of being
laughed at, scoffed at. Fear of scorn. Fear of not
being believed. Fear! It's all so *crazy!* When I'm in
a calm frame of mind I can sit down and think
things out logically, get things into perspective, and
then I know I'm loved by my folks — but I can't
feel that love inside me. It's all around me, *but I
can't feel it!* It's as if I'm at one end of a long, long
tunnel and the love is at the other end and we can't
seem to meet, to join, to unite. Oh, let me get far,
far, far from the madding crowd, or should I say
maddening crowd?

I loved it when I was a child and Daddy and I were
so close. He used to make me so happy. The
possessiveness of my love for him! The nights he
sat up with me holding me when I woke up from a
nightmare or from some unknown fear that would
get me in its grip and make my imagination go haywire. I would put my arms around him and cling
on to him tightly, and I'd feel safe and secure. He
would comfort me and hold me until I fell asleep
again. The happiness I received from him! The fun

we had. The laughter. The beautiful stories he used to make up and tell to me at night when I was tucked up in bed. I don't want to write about it — because what can a child do to make her father turn so indifferent and sort of cold towards her? It hurts too deeply to write about the happy times we had. Black out the hurt. Take some pills. My happiness now consists of round pills, long pills, pills the colour of the rainbow. Maybe I can climb onto that rainbow and find true happiness when I reach the end. I don't want a crock of gold. Just peace and happiness.

I suppose life, as most of us live it, is suffering. There is no denying the fact that as long as life is a sort of struggle, it cannot be anything but pain. Isn't that what a struggle means — the impact of two conflicting forces each trying to get the upper hand of the other?

Life is a series of choking knots that I want to unloosen, but my hands seem paralysed on the ropes. I must try and break through the brick wall I have built around myself, the defences; the world and I need each other. Without each other we lose all purpose. I wonder if I will still think so positively tomorrow, tonight, in an hour's time? Hope so, it's a nice feeling, 'cause I'm always thinking such *negative* thoughts.

Chapter 6

The Treatment

The first "fence" for any stolen goods of mine was a certain person (that I'm not going to identify) in St. Brendan's. The "deal" that I had going was that I would go out shoplifting for this person — jewellery, clothes, etc. — and in return would receive barbiturates, syringes, and needles.

But that wasn't my only source of supply. I was also friendly with quite a few of the nurses. I genuinely liked them — but that didn't stop me from using them. I used to help them make the beds, sort out the laundry, tidy the day-room (this was in the open unit), and do all kinds of messages for them. I suppose my work was put down as a kind of therapy. Anyway, roughly about four times a week one of the nurses used to go down to the surgery where all the medication, needles and syringes were kept, along with things like bandages and cotton wool and all that sort of stuff. She used to clean up the place and put things in order. One day I offered to go down with her and help her. So she said "fine, you'll keep me company anyway."

I kept her company, all right! I never stopped talking and chatting, so as to try and keep distracting her — which I succeeded in doing. I got her to let me help her clean out the cabinet where the drugs and syringes and spikes were kept. I took nothing the first time — nor the second, nor the third. I wanted her to trust me. It was always the same nurse, so I was okay. But the fourth time we went there, I took six syringes, a handful of needles, and a load of tablets. And the next time, and the next — and this went on for two whole months without anybody catching on!

Twice a week the nurses used to have to go to a central pharmacy to get medication that wasn't kept in the surgery in our own unit, or to stock up on regular medicines that were kept in the unit. Gradually, I fixed it so that I could go along with them. There were usually two or three heavy baskets for them to bring back, so I'd carry one basket. When the nurse would be reading out the list of drugs and so on that our unit had ordered, I'd wander casually into the back of the pharmacy, very innocent like, keeping up a non-stop chat with the pharmacist and nurse all the time. On several occasions I managed to come back out of that pharmacy loaded, and I don't just mean barbs — I got some pretty heavy gear, and syringes and spikes as well. Again, I was never caught.

They did have security procedures, of course, but nothing up to the standards of a hardened junkie. Only twice did I have a blood test taken, and a urine sample was taken once, the second time I was admitted. They only searched my room twice, although I was a known addict, in for the "cure".

When I robbed things in the hospital, I hardly ever shared out any of my gear to the other junkies there — syringes and spikes, yes, sometimes, but very, very rarely the junk I had ripped off.

* * *

One thing I will never forget about Brendan's was the food. A typical breakfast might consist of a hard-boiled egg (and I mean hard!), with four slices of brown bread — not four each, as there were four patients to each table — and plates and plates of soggy white bread, and porridge or cornflakes.

The high point of the luncheon menu would be scraps of meat surrounded by fat. It was quite a triumph when one eventually found the bit of meat after hacking away all the fat, with everything swimming in grease and a sort of white gravy, and lumpy potatoes and watery cabbage. They had a name for all this: "stew".

Chips, lost in a sea of grease. Fried egg swimming gallantly to try and stay afloat on top of the grease. Or maybe even another of those magnificent hard-boiled eggs. Not forgetting the inevitable pile of soggy white bread. "Tea."

About twice a week — I can't remember, it might have been more often — we used to have Chicken à la Scrag, or Chicken à la Squawk, depending on the vintage of the bird, not to mention the vintage of the cook! These chickens resembled nothing so much as anorexic seagulls. We used to have a shocking suspicion that the cooks went out with shotguns and massacred the hundreds of gulls that used to congregate behind one of the buildings where the waste food was dumped. I'll never forget going for walks up there, past the mounds of rotting food dumped on the ground behind one of the wards. The smell of decomposing cabbage — ugh! To take a walk up there, you'd think from the stench you were standing on the Liffey bed. Watching the seagulls hovering around like vultures was like being at a fishing port when the trawlers come in with their haul.

Any time a new patient came in, the questions they would inevitably ask the others would be "what's it like here, what are the staff like, what do you do all day?" — and "what's the food like?" To which one could only reply: Foul!

The menu never changed. Maybe a bit of variety has been added by now, but all the time I was there the meals were the same week in, week out. It has been well known for years that a healthy mind needs a healthy body. It has also been known that a lack of essential vitamins can play havoc with the mind. It can lead to severe depression, tension, anxiety, irritability, lack of concentration, listlessness and so on. You can have bad skin, you can be prone to all kinds of infections, prone to any bug going around, just because the body hasn't got the essential vitamins that it requires to carry on in a state of physical and mental well-being. How in God's name were people suffering from depression, tension etc., supposed to get their heads in order while living on the kind of diet that places like St. Brendan's used to offer while I was there?

Chapter 7

Introduction to Crime

I was into shoplifting for several years, starting when I was still a patient in the open unit of Brendan's.

It worked best when four of us would go shoplifting together. We always cleaned ourselves up and dressed pretty conservatively — at least in the beginning, before I got really bad. We would go into a store, and one or two of us would cause a disturbance, like faking a faint, or taking a fit. One guy used to go around the stores, rolling his eyes, carrying a large bible and shouting his head off: "Save your souls! Repent! Praise the Lord! Repent and save your souls! Alleluia, brothers, the Antichrist is with us! The time is near! Alleluia, brothers and sisters!" And he'd beat his chest and open up his bible and start shouting out passages from the Book of Revelations.

Strangely, this *always* worked. In fact he got quite a name for himself. The sales assistants in the stores used to laugh at him and call him "Alleluia the Mad Preacher", but they never seemed to suspect what he was up to.

Whoever created the disturbance always did it at one counter in the shop, while the rest of us spread ourselves around other counters containing things like electrical equipment, expensive clothes, china, antique articles, etc. We used to have bags that could be folded and made into shoulder bags, or sometimes maternity smocks over very wide slacks — but *never* jeans, never anything hip, trendy, way out, nothing to attract attention to ourselves. Sometimes we'd wear long, wide maternity dresses over jeans cut up to the knee, with four or five belts around the waist to hold the goods.

First we would buy something from a few of the counters in a big store, and ask the assistants' advice on things like make-up, coats, dresses or whatever. I don't know how much they suspected. While one of us would be talking to the sales assistant, another would be discreetly looking over valuable items in the store, and even more discreetly lifting a stash of things. But it was much easier when one of us would create a disturbance and a crowd would form around whichever person was fainting, throwing a fit or screaming blue murder that her bag had been robbed. Apart from those who actually went to help, the assistants at the other counters would also be interested in what was going on, and distracted from their counters, so we'd be able to help ourselves to some china, jewellery, clothes or electrical appliances.

The big stores were a cinch, especially at lunch-hour. Antique shops were like taking candy from a baby, only the candy wasn't sugar-coated but coated with money — and I *mean* real money! The large bookstores were simple, too. We'd come out in turns loaded with expensive books, and as for record shops and department stores that sold records, we must have ripped off literally *thousands* of discs and tapes. Most records are kept in their shelves, with only the sleeves out on display, but in some record shops, especially with bargain offers, the actual discs would be left in their covers, and those were the places we went for.

But the easiest robbing sprees of all were when we went off down the country. Unlike Dublin, none of our group was ever caught in the stores and small shops of country towns. We'd go down on the train for the day, and come back loaded with everything imaginable.

I'm not knocking the country, mind, just because their shops were so easy to do. The large chemists, for instance, were a dead cinch. I don't mean for knocking off drugs, but we got *tons* of make-up, perfume, talc sets and so on. We always went for the very best perfume and cosmetics. The security in those towns was practically nil — at least it was in those days. Clothes, china, shoes, antiques, you name it!

We'd leave a couple of empty suitcases hidden somewhere near the station when we'd arrive in one of those country towns, sometimes in a field, or even in the woods. And then, at the end of the day, when we would be getting the train again to go home to Dublin, we would find our suitcases, stuff them full of the stolen goods we had collected, and board the train for home.

Chapter 8

Portrait of Saint Brendan's written when I was sixteen

Destruction of self confidence.

Erosion of dignity.

Shameful lack of forward planning, for long stay patients, to help them go out into society again.

Disregard for the rights of individuals and parents in the application of "guinea-pig" treatment — L.S.D., Abreaction, etc.

Failure on the part of the majority of the staff to treat the patients as human beings who have personalities, feelings, fears and hopes.

Smug superiority of some of the hospital staff which inspires frustration and helpless fury.

Perpetuating an institutional system where boredom, loneliness and despair prevail.

Lack of a proper (recognised) system for lodging grievous complaints, airing legitimate grievances or proferring suggestions.

Being a patient in St. Brendan's is like living in the twilight zone. The clock stopped in the early nineteenth century. Time stood still and never moved forward. *Someone wind that clock!*

Chapter 9

From My Diary

Once upon a time, many years ago, two people came together in an act of love, and fused. Out of that act of love — a child, a daughter. A child to give delight, pleasure, happiness to this couple. *No!* Out of their love a problem was born. A mistake. A nuisance. A complication. A kaleidoscope of confusion. A fool. A mess. Oh, God, sort me out! I want my parents to be *proud* of me. I'm becoming a stranger to them. I want to get into a time tunnel and go back to when we were poor. I want to go back to when I was nine. Okay, so I was desperately unhappy at school, but home life was happy. Now it's tense and unhappy: but I am not the sole contributor.

I don't want to live. I don't want life. I don't want to live! I haven't wanted to live since I was

57

ten and nobody knows that. Nobody, except myself, my dog and God. Back, back, back to the womb. Then rebirth. Fresh. Clean. Clear. The resurrection of my soul. Powerful as an atomic explosion. Bigger, tumbling, twisting, slowly spiralling, bursting with the new-found energy it can no longer contain — reborn! If only, oh, if only! If pigs could fly and ducks could bark and dogs could talk and fairytales were true. If only.

> Red and yellow and pink and blue,
> I can see a rainbow, see a rainbow,
> See a rainbow too.

My life, myself, are contained within those red, yellow, pink, blue capsules. I'm beginning to notice that when I go for a week or two without taking any, I start feeling really weird — jumpy, hot and then cold, with *awful* pains in my stomach. Really sick. It's probably what my mother calls growing pains, the teenage blues.

> Yeah, man I've got de blues,
> The teenage blues,
> Oh, dem awful blues,
> Oh, dem awful blues,
> Dem awful blues are gonna go
> Cause I'm gonna pop some Glory Halleluia.

Have also started my period. That's why I feel peculiar. No longer a child now. I've joined the monthly road to motherhood. How awful. But, it's a bit odd that I should feel okay again as soon as I've popped a pill or two. All those symptoms go.

Violence breeds violence. So, tension, aggression and sarcasm must do likewise. Well, what with school and now home I'm going to sure grow up into one hell of an adult. Actually, I'm frightened to become adult, to "grow up". Oh, I don't want to remain thirteen for the rest of my life, but I'm so terrified of growing up, of maturing. I don't know why. Not knowing "why" to a lot of complications within myself frustrates me to screaming point.

Give me a rock, an oak tree, something strong and firm to lean on. I feel like wrapping Mammy in a box and marking it "Fragile, handle with care". She hurts so easily. I mean she gets hurt so easily and I can feel how she's feeling inside. It sort of transmits itself into me, and I cry inside for her. But I can't bring myself to show my feelings of understanding. When I feel the hurt she's going through, yes I do cry inside myself for her. But, for some reason, that's beyond my comprehension, I become cold, hostile, rude, and *very* hurtful towards her. I hate myself for it, but I hate feeling the desperate hurt in her. I feel so helpless. Oh, God what a mix-up. The hurt I put her through because I sort of feel, well, emotionally torn apart inside.

Creative expression is the need of my soul. Nature

— how I love you. God's creation. I feel so full at times of the beauty and wonder of his "tapestry" that I burst into tears. Tears of joy that I'm so lucky to be able to get completely in tune with nature. Tears of wonderment. Awe. The sea — its crashing fury against the rocks in a storm. The lightning shooting through the sky lighting the inky blackness for a few seconds like a neon light. The thunder keeping rhythm with the crashing booming waves. The seagulls screaming — soaring, soaring, diving, diving. Night orchestra. Who needs records when you can sit on a cliff and experience the strange calming effect of a wild storm?

The calmness of the sea. The stars almost reflected on the water. The moon making little shimmering lights here and there. The gentleness of the water as it laps against the pier. The silence broken only by the gentle ripple of the water. Nature stimulates me — imagine if I had not been gifted with such acute senses. How awful. Nature to me is like paradise. I want to open my heart and soul and bring the wonder and beauty and peace right inside me. It's so mystic. Stones, flowers, rivers, lakes. Everytime I look at flowers, stones, shells, I see new features in them. I never thought that the smallest, most familiar things were so inexhaustible in their possibilities.

Sunset. Oh, how beautiful. I just rush down to the beach, into the sea (jeans and all) and stretch my arms towards the sky. I feel that if I stretch long enough I can touch the sunset before it goes down — the golden rays shimmering on the water; the sky and sea lit up in a golden hue, uniting.

Dawn. Which is the most breath-taking? Sunset or sunrise? Neither. Each is unique. Go to the top of a hill at five and watch the dawn breaking. Slowly, oh so slowly, from darkness to a pink glow. Tinged with a milky whiteness. Spreading slowly over the sky, reflecting on the sea. To hear the first bird singing, then the second, then birds of all different types breaking into joyous song. Dawn chorus. I can see for miles and miles — oh, that sky! And the smell of freshness, of wild flowers, heather. The dew. Then the first car, then the milk-man — oh, well, better be going. Back to "civilisation"! I'd love to be Heidi or Tom Sawyer or the Borrowers.

Trees, leaves — what colours. Yellow leaves, green, brown, a mixture of brown and yellow. Those trees standing upright with their branches spreading outwards to protect me. Upwards to praise and thank God. Trees of *every* description and every colour. Old trees, new trees, young trees — all with a story to tell. All the seasons seem to blend into one — as far as the trees and leaves go — autumn, winter, spring, summer. It's incredible — incredulous! Rabbits hopping through the long grass, a squirrel — no, two squirrels. But, oh, the singing of the birds! Now the pink and white sky has changed to a mist and I can no longer see for miles. But who cares, I'm in nature. Nature is in *me!* The rain lashing down, soaking me — people running for shelter -- not me. I walk ever so slowly enjoying the feel of the pelting rain. The wind. That powerful force, howling through the trees, reaching a crescendo, then dying down, then *slowly* reaching a pitch again.

Oh, there's so much to see and feel that I get bewildered by it all. Woods, mountains, wilderness, flowers, cliffs, the sea, moon, sun, stars, night, day, sunrise, sunset, dawn, storms, shells, lakes, rivers, rain, birds, leaves, the seasons, trees. Oh, to live in the country. Ah, well, I'm lucky to live so near the sea and cliffs. I can't have everything, though I would love everything nature has to offer. Peaceful eternity.

Artistic, creative people are supposed to be temperamental. The three things go together. Well, I'm artistic, creative, so naturally I'm temperamental, and soul searching. Though I think maybe that's just an excuse for my anti-social behaviour.

Oh, God, repressed anger and hurt can sure be damaging to the mind and soul. When the fighting begins, or rather the one-way fight, I feel so helpless! Caught up in the middle. Then I start to feel angry, then sort of all tight and knotted up inside, frustrated, 'cause I don't know how to help. Oh, I know I have written these feelings, these thoughts before, but I *have* to keep writing them down -- it's a sort of release for me.

How do I stop you, Daddy, shouting, talking

through clenched teeth, hurting, being sarcastic, oh, so sarcastic? And you, Mammy, crying, your eyes full of hurt, your voice full of hurt and pain? If both of you had any idea of how I feel. Daddy, the tension inside you, that awful high-pitched tension, your frustration and verbal violence, it gets inside me. Your intense tension and hurtfulness makes *me* feel violent, tense, as well as the sheer helplessness and hopelessness I feel when the shouting and crying begin. The one-sided arguments — and they are so childish, so futile.

The violence that gets inside me is violence directed first at both of you, then at myself. I couldn't hurt people, not hurt them physically anyway. Verbally, yes. So I lash into myself.

I feel foolish when I write down what I really feel. There was, and still is, a time when I was afraid to express myself. Then a time when I talked, said what I felt and asked for that in return. Spacer (he's dead now) I knew there was something he understood — but I wasn't sure what it was ... Then I thought maybe he was just another person, another junkie. I was saying "This is me." But it was different somehow, not so desperate. I could feel him saying all the time "Calm down, don't yell, I know it's you and this is me." And then I knew it was me he understood. Then I became less disorientated and more aware.

I want to smash everything in sight. Cause destruction everywhere. Slash myself to pieces. Cut my throat from ear to ear. Set fire to myself. And I'm not being melodramatic. Oh, Jesus Christ, will you *help* me. Why should you, though? I'm not much of a child of yours to be proud of, am I?

Oh, hell, I can't relate!

I don't think I'm frustrated because I'm violent. I'm violent because I'm so full of frustration! All my hate is repressed hate, sort of displaced anger and hate. Oh, yes, repressed anger and hate certainly can be damaging! It's bugging me that I can get violent and angry without cause (subconsciously of course, there's a cause). It's becoming like a habit. Yes! I have had you, anger, for so long that I don't know what it's like not to have you. Oh, somebody, anybody, hold me tight. Dispel my fears. Love me.

One can't feel content and secure just walking along thinking about oneself, even in the most serene, pure place, unless one can accept oneself as part of it and accept its feelings, not force its feelings. I regret not being able to express this properly, perhaps some other time. It's only when you know life that there is no fear of death. But I am (part of me) afraid of death 'cause I know nothing about life. Not *real* life. When I'm unsure I must make myself sure. When I'm sure I must hold my ground, and remember that the strongest building has an amount of play so that it may sway with more powerful forces. The rigid building is the weakest for it will crack and fall under strain. Simplicity is the most complex. If you keep putting one foot forward, you'll travel around the world. That's idealistic. But what's wrong with high ideals?

I'm gonna go nuts. I've got to stop thinking for a while — be a void. How quickly my moods change. The discontent with myself, with life — this lack of interest is spreading like a cancer. So I'll arrest it, before it kills me emotionally — I'll arrest it with my "mother's little helpers". My bottles of little coloured pills. My beautiful rainbow. *My* reality!

Tonight I was given a tiny little tablet and oh, God, I think it's making me go crazy. If I feel sane in the morning I will write down what that tablet made me see. It's morning and I still feel a bit weird. Everything looks distorted. Last night there were huge rats and mice and half-eaten people in my room. Dead people standing beside my bed leering down at me, their faces half-eaten away. Big skulls with maggots and worms crawling out of them. I kept trying to scream for help, but no sound would come. The noise of the cars and buses outside seemed to have got right into my head and was echoing; all sound took on the sound of an echo. Then I actually saw inside my head — I did — and there were little insects and fleas and long white worms entwined around one another; then they came apart and started to crawl around my brain. I tried to bang my head, but I seemed to have become paralysed. That's all I remember — I think I might have passed out either from terror or from the tablet. Must find out what it was. How could such a tiny little thing make me feel so crazy! And those awful, oh God, those horrific things I saw. How could it?

When something is going to happen — maybe you're even sure it's going to happen — you have got to realise that that something is inevitable, so don't force it before its time. Things just happen no matter what. So, I must not force things before their time, 'cause I'm always doing that. Oh for God's sake what unadulterated rubbish I write! I write exactly what I am — rubbish, of no use to anyone, except the binmen and then — even then — I'm of no use to them. I'm a bleeding mass of self pity! Just give over and cop on to yourself — grow up ... No! No, not just yet, not just yet. I'm still too afraid to enter the "adult world".

Chapter 10

Back in Brendan's

My second admission to Brendan's was horrific, to say the least. I was seriously addicted, disturbed, very wild, very unhappy, with an intense fear and hatred of people. When I came out of that hospital for the second time, I was still on drugs, unhappy, bitter, suspicious of kindness and gentleness, still wild, and with an intense fear and loathing of Brendan's and of the whole psychiatric system.

Did I get any help there? Well, for the first few weeks, yes. Then things got out of hand. I actually became dependent on the hospital though I hated it. I started inventing problems, and when I told my doctor this, she just said: "Lisa, when your addiction is under control, then, and only then, can you go." Jesus Christ, I was hardly *ever* off junk in that place!

Soon after that, there was no need to invent

problems, because I suffered a serious nervous breakdown. Oh man, imagine having a nervous breakdown in a psychiatric hospital! The mind boggles. I developed problems I never had. The only reason I stayed with that psychiatrist was out of loyalty, but my fear of her grew like a cancer.

In Brendan's they had a habit of locking patients up. Is this what psychiatrists learn during their training? To treat their patients with threats? To keep them in a constant state of anxiety? Is this how patients make their "recovery"? Through fear of fear? I was never an acute anxiety case before Brendan's. I am one now. Is the only solution for a patient who attempts suicide, refuses to eat, becomes hysterical and doesn't "conform": to lock them in a ward with mentally unbalanced patients? To lock them up with patients who have been there twenty, thirty years? A long day-room — patients walking up and down, up and down, talking to themselves, breaking windows, attacking one another. The ward. Oh God! A ward with beds practically on top of one another. A ward of filth and squalor. Of hopelessness, despair, apathy, screaming and howling like wild animals — animals in pain. Of windows being broken day and night. Patients beating up the staff, staff being cruel to patients. The smell of unwashed bodies. The smell of urine in the day room and in the ward. The incoherent rambling night and day. Mealtimes like the mad hatter's party. The constant jangling of those goddamned keys that all senior nurses seem to have attached to their uniforms. Enough to drive anyone mad. But the screams, oh God, the screams of emotional pain, of tortured minds and souls. Jesus!

To be fair to the people who locked me up in the closed wards, the only time I was off drugs in that hospital was when I was locked up! While I was just attending the hospital for treatment, at the age of fifteen and again at seventeen, I was able to sleep rough, crash in on my friends' pads, live as a squatter, go off to England, get pulled in by the police, even practise prostitution for three months. And I was always able to keep up my drug habit — all the time I was a patient. Sick!

I was locked up in the really bad ward for running away, and for constantly taking drugs. Patients have been in that ward for up to twenty years. Sometimes longer. I was only fifteen years old when I was first locked up. Dear God, I shall *never* forget the experience. It seems to be an occupational hazard for some doctors — locking patients up. Is it a means of punishment, or what?

Those patients *never* receive a visitor. Never. How the hell can they be released to a "half way house" (a psychiatric hostel in the grounds of Brendan's)? That life and that ward is all they know. They are a danger to themselves, and some are a danger to society — or would be if let out. It's so sad, but the ward will never be levelled to the ground — high ideals, a brilliant idea, but impossible to put into practice. Anyway, that kind of talk has been going on for years, and that's all it is. Talk! As far as the dangerous wards are concerned, anyway.

I was lucky. I had a nurse with me night and day, so I could get out of that hell hole, into the grounds. Also, being the youngest there, I was the "pet" of the ward. Ugh! I suppose the psychiatrist that put me there thought I would attempt suicide, and that's why she had me watched. I also had privileges that none of the other poor unfortunates had.

I'll say one thing though, the patients were very kind to me and I was very fond of them, though terrified of the majority of them.

The only time I was off drugs was when I was locked up in the bad ward — the snake pit! What a place! What a form of punishment!

The worst thing that ever happened to me in that ward was when it was decided that I should go cold turkey. It was okay for the first three days. Then, Oh God, my head blew open, I kept smashing myself off the walls, I started to hallucinate, became desperately paranoid, broke into frightful sweats, got headaches, shaking, blackouts, smashing my head off anything hard. I was put in a room, with a bed covered in some sort of material, as were the walls, so that I wouldn't harm myself. Harm myself! I took a fit so bad that I ended in the Mater completely paralysed down one side, and my jaw had locked. I remained like that for a week.

I still had to go back to the locked ward, though,

when I was physically able, but they put me on a substitute drug to prevent a recurrence of the horror of the fits and the horror of going cold turkey.

Have you ever seen an addict go through cold turkey? It's horrific. Roughly about ten hours after the drug has worn off — morph or heroin — you begin to feel very uneasy. You sweat, yawn, shiver all at the same time. You become extremely weak. A watery discharge pours from your eyes. You fall into an abnormal sleep — tossing, restless.

When waking after sixteen to twenty hours after the last fix of the drug, you enter your personal hell. Watery mucus pours from the nose. The pupils become very dilated. The skin is freezing. Your bowels act with incredible violence. You then have violent vomiting, which becomes stained with blood. Abdominal pain is severe and increases rapidly. As many as forty or fifty large stools are passed in a day. About thirty-four to thirty-six hours after the last fix the addict presents a frightful spectacle. The whole body twitches and the legs kick involuntarily. Throughout this whole period, it's impossible to sleep. The muscles keep going into painful cramps. The sweating is unbelievable. Filthy, sweaty — you present a subhuman appearance; eyes sunken into the back of the head, covered with your own vomit, urine and faeces. You can lose as much as twelve pounds, as you neither eat nor drink. This withdrawal usually lasts for about eight to nine days — if your heart can stand up to it. Otherwise you have a stroke, become mentally unhinged, or die.

When I eventually was allowed to go back to the open ward, which was paradise to me now, I was bitter, highly nervous and trusted nobody. I was also under constant threat of the locked ward if I "misbehaved". I never did go back to that ward, but my drug abuse got worse, and I got wilder — and I was supposed to be in that hospital for help with my addiction. Hospital! Jesus Christ!

I had made friends with four other addicts in the open ward, and one of them showed me how to inject. Addicts are incredibly resourceful, and getting access to drugs in a hospital was no problem for this girl. She took me under her wing. Ironic, wasn't it? My first fix in a psychiatric hospital! At fifteen-and-a-half years old.

Chapter 11

Acid Trip

When I was sixteen, I had got into acid, and got into it very heavily. Jesus, the trips were mind-blowing. I think that in all my years of acid dropping, I had only six or seven good trips. How I didn't end my days in a padded cell is something I'll never know. I used to run down O'Connell Street screaming that there were devils and dead people after me, or huddle up in a corner of some street absolutely *petrified* of anyone who came near me, but, inside, screaming for help. The police always brought me back to Brendan's. Then I started running down to either the Bridewell or Mountjoy police station and smashing the windows out of sheer terror. Funny enough, the police were kind to me and never roughed me up.

For about two years after my second trip I thought I had the devil in me, and I used to scream and scream for a priest to get the devil out of me.

I used to have to cut my arms open to try and get the worms and long white squiggly things out of my arms. I'd tear at my face 'cause there were *huge* flies and maggots crawling over my face. Sometimes, when I'd look in the mirror, I'd see a woman of about seventy or ninety. I still get the occasional flashback, especially when I am under stress and strain, or under disco lighting.

When I was in Brendan's for the second time, my mind had gone haywire from acid. Nothing or nobody could convince me that I wasn't in a concentration camp. I got it into my head that one of the sisters in charge of the unit I was in was an escaped Nazi in disguise. So I used to go down to the police — without breaking their windows this time — begging them to arrest her and put her on trial. They used to humour me, until it got out of hand. I used to run to the Bridewell cop station or Mountjoy, screaming at the cops to take her away. She *was* a Nazi, she *was!* I was put under heavy sedation for a week or two and when my psychiatrist told me what I had been doing, I refused to believe her — I couldn't remember anything at all. But I still had a horror and an intense fear of that nurse.

One of my favourite pastimes in Brendan's was breaking windows. I used to do it first out of sheer boredom, then I noticed it got rid of a lot of pent-up frustration and tension and seemed to ease the turmoil inside of me. Just the feeling of smashing my fist through a window, or my shoe, and hear the glass breaking. I remember at times when I used to do it I'd think to myself, scream silently inside, "Jesus, Jesus Christ! I'm supposed to be in here for a 'cure', and I'm out of my head day and night on drugs. What kind of hospital is this? What kind of doctors are you all? None of you give a shit!"

After a while, the unit I was in looked like Long Kesh. The day after the windows were broken they would be boarded up for about two days. Then new windows would be put in — but not for long. They'd soon be out again! And the boards would be put up again. It looked awful. And this was the "exclusive" unit of Brendan's. Exclusive! Ha! I used to go down to the lower house — that was what the wards, the locked wards, were called — and smash windows there, and also the shop window and the windows in the hall where they used to hold dances. But as the windows in those places were always broken, a few more broken windows didn't make much difference to the appearance of the place. Anyway, those wards needed fresh air badly to get rid of the stench of urine, stale urine, unwashed bodies, vomit etc., etc. — but *that* wasn't my intention. I'm all for human rights, now, but then I was just for myself. There was no charitable motive behind my smashing of the windows in the locked wards. When I was locked up in those wards it was in the winter, and I thought it was very funny to see the nurses' caps "taking sail", as they passed by the broken windows, when a gush of wind blew into the dayroom.

For as far back as I can remember there has been talk of "pulling the lower houses down". Integrating the patients into our so-called society. All very well in theory, but *not* in practice. In the "lower house" there were men and women who were admitted when medicines and other kinds of treatment for people who were — I refuse to say "sick in the mind" — deeply disturbed, had not reached the stage of advancement they now have. Teenagers, young adults, middle-aged men and women were dumped in there and called "mental". Group therapy and group sessions were alien. Padded cells and strait-jackets were commonplace. Those patients know no other kind of life.

The psychiatric system stinks! Like I said, if you can't pay £130 a week for St. Patrick's, you have a choice of Brendan's, Loman's, Hospital 6 in St. James's, or Portrane. Actually, you don't really have a choice. It all depends on which catchment area you are in — so you're lucky if you live in the catchment area for Hospital 6! At least they genuinely care about you there. There's not much difference between the other hospitals. If you are submissive, show a very limited intelligence, or none at all, you do fine. You'll be treated pretty okay. Any sign of aggression — speaking up for yourself — and you're sunk. Is it resentment on the part of the psychiatrists? Or what in God's name is it? Why do they want us walking around like zombies, doped up with medication that half of us don't even need?

Chapter 12

Prostitution

My first introduction to prostitution came in Brendan's, from the same girl who showed me how to "fix" with a needle. I was in the open unit of the hospital, and among the patients attending there were a lot of "high society" men who had suffered nervous breakdowns due to marital problems, overwork, etc. I had sex with five of them. We used to meet outside the unit. I hated it. I felt nothing for those men. They felt nothing for me. I just needed money for drugs, they just wanted to satisfy their sexual appetite.

Well, I certainly got enough money! One man gave me forty pounds, another fifty-four pounds. But one man refused to give me anything at all, after he had used my body brutally.

Anyway, I got enough money from those people to buy my tabs of acid and my barbs, which at the time I was into very heavily — although I had to give half of everything I earned to my friend — let's call her Deirdre — who acted as the go-between. I also managed to score a few tabs of speed.

After leaving Brendan's, I continued "on the game" for nearly a year. My boyfriend of the time was the one who introduced me to the sleazy world of real prostitution, on a regular basis, in a certain area of Dublin. I was getting enough money off these men to keep me supplied with gear, and keep my habit going. It was a soul-destroying experience. John, my boyfriend, used actually get guys to come up to his flat and then leave us together. One thing in my favour, though — I was always so spaced out of my mind that I was only vaguely aware of what those men did to me — but I was aware enough to feel sickened, disgusted, degraded.

Sometimes, in one week, I would earn from £150 to £300 — part of which went on drugs, and the rest would be taken by John.

I really loved that guy. Physically, mentally, emotionally. I loved him. When my parents met him, they told me "he's weird, there's something about him we just can't take to." Of course they had no idea of our real relationship, and anyway at sixteen, seventeen years of age who's going to take any notice of their parents? I knew he loved me, but I just didn't understand how messed up he was inside.

Even when John got me into the filthy world of

prostitution, I thought it was just because he loved me so much that he didn't want to see me going through the agonies of withdrawals because I wouldn't have the money to score off the pushers. It was easier than shoplifting, anyway, and brought in a hell of a lot more money. "Love is blind." *How true!*

When he didn't bring the men up to his flat, I used to go down and stand on the footpath outside the house. The street was well known for prostitutes — there would be two girls across the road from where I stood, and maybe two more further up the street, with another group down at the corner. Some nights there'd be no business, but all in all business was good. There was certainly no shortage at weekends. When I was picked up on the street I would usually be brought to some place like a hotel or boarding house, but other times they would take me to a flat. (It wouldn't be the men's own flats, though, just a place on loan from some "friends" for the night). Sometimes I'd get my money in advance, but usually after. There was hardly ever any conversation, either before or after — except once, a man simply wanted to talk, and talk he did: non-stop until dawn! He gave me a bundle of notes, forty-eight pounds just for listening to him. It was all about his wife. I think I spoke about four times during the night.

I never hung around the best-known red-light districts — only one place, at John's flat. Some of the men he would bring up would be in their late fifties, others in their forties or even middle thirties. On one occasion a man, probably going on sixty, wanted me to hit him with chains and a stick, and do some other incredibly sickening things to him, to arouse him sexually. He didn't want me to go to bed — just do weird things to him. God forgive me, I did what he wanted, and got paid an enormous amount of money. Most of them, naturally, just wanted plain straightforward sex. I didn't do that much "business", but I still made £50, £70, even £90 a night. So for a year and three months I was never short of money for drugs. Then, in the end, I got so sickened at what I had sunk to, and so disgusted with sex itself, that I refused to do it any more. So I went back to shop-lifting, begging, breaking and entering, forging scripts and stealing syringes and other stuff from casualty wards, in order to pay for my habit.

Only once in my fifteen months of prostitution did I get seriously beaten up. I got a bruised body, a black eye and a neck all covered in long scratches. I had taken a lot of gear that day, and when I was picked up during the night and taken to a flat somewhere, I just fell into a deep sleep, *on*, not in, the bed. The man, whoever he was, obviously couldn't wake me, and when I woke up next morning there was no sign of him, but I was black and blue — my payment for the night!

Chapter 13

The Commune

It was around this time that my boyfriend, John, introduced me to some people that were living together in a big house out in one of the southside suburbs, and I started visiting there, and making friends with the inhabitants, until eventually I moved in with them.

There were ten of us staying in the commune, and the others were mildly into gear. It was simply an "image", a fun thing, with some of them, just like it had been with me, but slowly, one by one, they started getting into hard drugs and I was no longer the only total drug addict crashing there. It was only a matter of time anyway for their addiction to set in. You can't experiment with hard drugs and not become addicted.

In all honesty, I can't say that we didn't have

some good times, and a lot of fun, in that commune, before the dirt and squalor set in, when the others became hard drug addicts like me.

It was a huge old house, and we painted the rooms in lurid colours. We thought the colour scheme was beautiful. Looking back now it was — well — I just can't put into words just what it *was* like. The ceilings were purple and red. One wall in the main room was painted in two different shades of red, another wall was light and dark purple. On a third wall one of the guys had painted a huge mural — totally abstract. The bathroom was red and the kitchen was red, white and purple. As if that wasn't bad enough, we had a pet dog, and we dyed a green and purple streak from his neck to his tail. He looked fabulous. The only one of us who did!

We had speakers rigged up in *all* the rooms, so there was music everywhere. Oh, I was so happy there. But that kind of happiness never lasts, thank God. But I *was* genuinely happy there for a long time. I'm full of contradictions over life in the commune. It wasn't all drug-induced happiness either. Now this was before the others got heavily into drugs and started mainlining. They used to just drop tabs of acid and smoke dope, now and then. Then they got into acid very heavily and were constantly either on a bad trip or on the rare good trip. Then they got into barbs, and cocaine, morphine and heroin. I still stayed there, though by now the house was a health hazard. It was filthy.

But before all that set in, it was a great place. I'm not going on a sentimental blind journey into the past. I can only tell it the way it was. The house was a mixture of Carnaby Street, the Dandelion Market and the Far East — excluding the colour scheme, of course! It was, in all honesty, a hippies' paradise, and that suited us right down to the ground. Right down to the jangling bangles on our ankles.

We never seemed to sleep. Most nights we'd go to the sea and sit around talking or listening to the guys playing guitars. One guy was brilliant on the flute and to hear him play in the silence at three in the morning on the beach was breathtaking. Or we'd all run into the sea in jeans and tee shirts and swim until we were exhausted.

Other times we'd sit on the steps of the house talking, laughing, acting the fool until morning, then we'd set up the stereo and amp and blast the house with sounds. Or we'd go and have breakfast in Bewley's and spend the rest of the day on the Green — in between scoring whatever we were into at the time. For me it was acid, speed and barbs. For the others, acid and dope. We also spent time shoplifting and ripping off handbags in restaurants and hotels. There always seemed to be a party going on. And on, and on! We would provide a massive curry and everyone could go down to the kitchen and help themselves. We'd usually finish off the party by piling into cars and going off to the sea. We'd have dancing and singing on the beach — the beach we always went to, whether it was just the ten of us, or whether it was after a party and there would be up to thirty people, was nowhere near any houses and so we *never* disturbed anybody. The thing we enjoyed most was a sort of Zorba the Greek dance — round and round the bonfire and into the sea, or, that old fashioned dance, the Conga. *That* was great! Thirty people weaving their way up and down the beach, kicking their legs to the right, then to the left, round and round. It was just so sad that we were always out of our heads on something — 'cause you can have that kind of fun without being on *anything!*

The man and woman who owned the house were real characters. They were married, but she had a boyfriend, I should say *man* friend, living in the house. And he had a girlfriend. Both living in the house. It had been going on long before any of us got to know them! They were middle-aged self-styled hippies.

Her room was like something out of the Victorian era. She used to spend the day reclining on her bed, sipping wine and popping the odd barbiturate. All that was needed to complete the Cleopatra character she had adopted was the lover feeding her grapes. She would get up around 3.30 or four o'clock and glide downstairs. She had a magnificent command of English and could converse on any subject. She used to have us spellbound listening to her. She also had a tremendous sense of humour and could relate funny incidents from her past that would have us convulsed with laughter. She was also as wild and mad as we were! She always came to life at night — a bit like Dracula — and would think up the maddest, zaniest, escapades for all of us — the husband and mistress, herself and her lover included.

We went up the Dublin Mountains at three in the morning and the fellows would bring guitars, tin whistles, a banjo, flute and a set of drums. We'd go near the Hellfire Club and have a jazz session. Another time we went streaking at two in the morning up the road, across a field and back again and then put on jeans and sweat shirts and went out to the sea, stripped off and ran naked into the sea and then up and down the beach. We were all out of our heads on gear, of course.

The filth, dirt, stench got to me eventually. Guys used the hallway as a toilet. There were also a few people into black magic in a big way.

I was put into the centre of a circle of about eight, and they started chanting — this was to get the "devil" out of me. Just like school all over again! Then they all joined hands and started going around me faster and faster, keeping up their weird chant. Then they flung blood at me.

At one corner of the room one young girl was doing the ouija board, and the glass kept going round to the devil, and then death. Anytime she used to do the board she'd pass out and go into a deep sleep. Another girl was into the tarot cards in a very big way. When she did them with me the card of death *always* came up.

I passed out when they flung the blood at me and then they started to cover me with blood on my forehead. At four in the morning the house would go icy cold. Freezing. And the hairs on the dog would stand up and he'd go tearing around the house barking. The blood they used to put on me was their own. They would slash their legs and I'd get their blood flung at me and then a cross of blood on my forehead. On four occasions I had to drink an egg cup of blood. The awful thing was that I fully believed in what they were doing — that they could get the "devil" out of me.

Then I started getting into the whole act, and we used to pick a girl or guy, whoever was willing, to stand in the middle of the room, while we circled around, chanting. As I was supposed to have the devil in me still, I was made to cut myself viciously — which I did. I'd slash my arms until there was enough blood to fill a tea cup. What I didn't know — though I had a peculiar feeling about it — was that the leader of the group, a tough weirdo, was actually praying to the devil, and this was really devil-worship. We were all scared of this guy.

Even now, sometimes when I have a flashback I think everybody is the devil and I must have sex with the devil and give birth to devils so that they can take over the world and (it's a *horrible* feeling) I have to be the mother of all the devils and people must pray to me.

What brought me to my senses in my blown-out

mind, was one day when the group leader brought home a huge painting of the devil, with the feet crushing God (I guess) and a chicken — a real chicken. He killed the chicken in front of us and then made us drink the blood. Then he went back to the huge grotesque painting and, kneeling, held up the chicken, saying: "Oh, Lord, devil of all devils, I bring to you your first of many sacrifices." He then started up an eerie chant, bowing and spreading himself out on the floor, then kissing the feet of the devil.

We were all pretty shook-up and frightened. So it was this, as well as the stench, dirt and so on, that made me decide to leave early the next morning. I never returned to the house.

I split from the scene there and started dossing around. I was in a complete world of my own. As soon as I'd get a fix or pill I'd just wander around town or go down the country, then come back to the dealers for the next fix or pill. I had stopped going round with the other addicts. I just kept to myself, becoming more and more apathetic and needing a larger dose each time I fixed or dropped tabs. Sleeping in fields, on the beach, in toilets — anywhere. I even hid in a confession box one night when they were closing the church for the night. I slept there for the night and sneaked out when the church was re-opened the following morning.

I'd no interest in food, but if I wanted something to eat I just had to walk into a small shop, grab a loaf of bread and butter and run. Easy enough, too, to rob a knife in a hotel or restaurant. Restaurants were the easiest! I also used to go into cake shops, calmly stack up with goodies and run — and I mean *run!* I was never caught.

I looked like a down and out, which in fact I was. My hair was tangled and filthy. I was covered in boils and septic spots. My weight was down to seven stone three. My teeth were black, with bits of enamel falling out. I smelt worse than I looked. Some people would give a slight shudder when I passed them by. Others would give a violent shudder!

I was really losing my grip. Soon I couldn't fend for myself any longer, out on the streets.

My next trip to a mental hospital was a step up in the world — up from the common herd of St. Brendan's to the more select surroundings of St. Patrick's. Just like back in my schooldays, I was once again joining the club for the élite.

At £130 a week, St. Patrick's was like a Grade A luxury hotel, reserved for the higher social classes on their VHI insurance. I felt out of place there, yet it is the finest hospital, you get the best of treatment. What a split! St. Pat's for the well-off, Brendan's or Loman's for the lower income bracket.

Chapter 14

From My Diary

Brought here in a state of complete nervous breakdown.

Wednesday
Became a patient in St. Patrick's today. I'm slowly cracking up. Mind is being blown to pieces. Hey! Who am I?

Thursday
Saw Dr. A. On heavy sedation. Slept a lot. My mother came in, and Carla.

Friday
Saw Dr. B, Dr. A and a student. Maureen and Jack came in to see me. Another man came up to the ward — had a long chat with me about gestalt therapy. Wish someone would tell me where I am and who I am!

From My Diary

Saturday
Slept.

Sunday
Slept.

Monday
Saw Professor C, Dr. A and the student. Slept. Went to the therapy group. Came back. Slept. Slept. Slept.

Tuesday
Saw Dr. A — she's a great doctor and I like her nearly, only nearly, as much as Dr. D. Went to group. An amazing experience, and the leader is a fascinating man. Saw my student — poor guy, he thinks I'm crazy! He's right! Had visitors. Elizabeth split — more power to her! They're watching me like a hawk, but I'm too doped with sedation to run even as far as the door of the ward.

Friday — I mean Wednesday
Saw Dr. A. Saw my student — he's frightening me. He keeps looking worried at things I tell him, and he's asking me the most peculiar questions. I think he has me labelled as paranoid and God knows what, but I wish he would keep his diagnosis to himself. He doesn't know who I am either; he knows my name, everyone does — even me — but nobody can tell me who I am! Can anybody understand what I'm asking? WHO AM I? WHO AM I?

Oh, man, I need a fix!!

Thursday
Saw Dr. A. I feel sick. No group. Had visitors. It's a pity everyone is dead, I have no one to talk to. Well, I talk to them, but I don't like talking to dead people. Of course, I have to act normal, pretend they are alive, it's horrible! All this because I over-dosed on acid!

Still feel very sick. Sort of disjointed — not me. Had visitors. Oh, God, I'm in a horrible living nightmare. Do I have a father? What's a mother? Saw Grandad — he's been dead seven years — wish he'd go away. I must die. Yes, I've got to. I'VE GOT TO DIE. I'm being pulled by another part of me.

Tried to kill myself last night. God, why don't you want me to die? Why won't you let me? I could have died last night, you *know* that, but you didn't let me! Do you not want me? Blood. Blood. Blood. Everywhere. All over the place. All over me. All over the nurses, the night sister, the doctor. Blood; blood everywhere. Awful. Horrible. WHEN WILL THIS NIGHTMARE END? I'm so tired. Damn the tablets. They're doing me harm. So is Dr. A and the therapist and Dr. B and Dr. X.

Saw Dr. A and Dr. B and my student — oh, I wish he would leave me alone! Went to group. Very good. Pity the tranquillity doesn't last! This business of being brought everywhere with a nurse is getting on my nerves. I feel like a prisoner.

Ran away today. Got as far as the gates — big deal! When I said I'd behave myself the four nurses let go of their grip on me and I made off again, tore off down Thomas Street, into town, and then I hadn't a clue where I was. The noise! Went into a police station. Took them an hour to find out who I was and where I was from. Everything had gone blank on me. Brought back to hospital. Put to bed. Was given two injections.

Saw Dr. A. Got into trouble for running away — I didn't actually run away, I just panicked and ran. I didn't know where I was running to, I just ran. They have hidden cameras and mikes all over the place, but I don't know who is planting them. Someone or something is trying to take me over. An Alien Force? The cameras take films of my mind and the mikes take readings of my brain and transmit them somewhere — where, though? I MUST MAKE MY MIND A BLANK.

Keep seeing dead people, bats, seagulls, shadows, hostility and hatred towards me from everyone. Walked with death today. Everyone and everything looked distorted. Sat down on one of the seats in the hall and only living people could sit on my right side. I had to tell those who sat on the left side of me to go away. They were dead. Oh, they looked awful. Skulls, with worms crawling out of what used to be their eyes and big open spaces with teeth rotting where their mouths used to be. I couldn't stop screaming — I had to scream that only living people could sit beside me — screaming, screaming, screaming. Got another injection. I think sometimes that these injections are meant to slowly kill me. To make me one of these living dead that are taking over the world.

One doctor is out to destroy me. Every morning he pats me on the shoulder and by doing that he destroys a part of me each day. By touching me he draws a source of my life into him, leaving me drained of life's energy. It's my life force he wants.

Didn't see Dr. A today. Don't mind. I'm too depressed to talk. I'm a bit frightened of her.

Saw Dr. A, she couldn't stay very long. I know she's very busy and she's great to see me every day. I'm not going to think about the end of the year. Another shrink! Oh, God, Dr. D, I'll never forget you. If I start dwelling on him, I'm going to cry. I never cry here, except in group sessions.

I don't know the day or date. I think it's Saturday. Ruth, Dympna, Ursula, Freda, Pierce and Ann and David and Peter and Gloria came in. My mother came in later on. I feel kinda well and wanted.

There's a lot of people standing outside the window, only Dr. B, Dr. A and my student say they are not there. That there is nobody, definitely nobody outside the window. But I know they are there! Why do people lie to me? Why must they? Grandad is sitting on the bed beside me. My Grandad has come back to life 'cause he loved me so much. I guess he wants to take me back to death with him. I love — loved my Grandad — no, not past tense, present tense — love! I would like to go with him.

Oh, I'm frightened. My eyes are coming out of their sockets. I saw them coming out when I was looking in the mirror — if I stare long enough I can see myself changing. Eyes coming out. Head becoming a skull. Worms eating me. Smash the window, smash the mirror, smash it, smash myself changing — blood all over my hands, face, hair. Stitches. Two injections. Very sleepy.

I won't eat! I won't. I WON'T! Oh, these stupid tablets and injections are stopping me doing what I want to do. They're slowing down my impulsiveness. I wish the other person inside me would go! She's evil, destructive and she's destroying me — the good, nice part of me.

I feel like harming myself. I don't want to do anything — no, I do! But I don't. Oh, help me somebody. That destructive person (self destructive) wants to make me harm myself but she's not going to get hold of me. I'm going to tell the nurse how I feel.

I ate two meals today and didn't make myself sick, but I got so aggressive and, for the first time in my life, I directed it outwards, not towards myself. But I didn't direct it outwards in a constructive way. I shouted at sister and Dr. B and the student doctor and it was getting worse and worse and I wanted to strike anyone who came near me. I got so depressed! I hated everyone. I was breaking out in a cold sweat from aggression and agitation. I told Dr. B and he gave me two tablets. I was okay after a while, but very sleepy, Dr. B said that the food caused all the problems and that I must keep eating in order to break that link.

Today I ate again and the same thing happened, except that I directed the negativity towards myself this time. When they unlocked the ward door I ran out of the ward and into the grounds. It was dark, and I smashed and smashed my head off the wall. The nurses found me and brought me back to the ward, fixed my forehead which was badly grazed, and my face. Saw some doctor who sedated me. I will not eat again. I cried today in front of everyone, but I didn't care, I felt and feel so unhappy. There's nothing to live for. Nothing! Nothing! There's no future — just a long, long, black tunnel with no light at the end.

From My Diary

Why won't my Dad come in to see me? There's a big lump of hurt inside me and it's smothering me.

Saw Dr. A. I think she's a bit unbalanced, so I will go along with everything she says. I don't want to be the cause of her going over the edge. It's laughable. There's nothing wrong with me. I'm well but *she's* sick. Nobody seems to see this. I don't want a sick psychiatrist. I don't want a disturbed psychiatrist. I will tell the therapist she's not well and then I will leave this place. I think it's a hospital. I'm not sure. I feel very confused. Dr. A doesn't look like the Dr. A I used to see before — so, who is she?

I keep my eyes fixed on that door at visiting time, hoping, praying and willing Dad to walk in. I'd love to feel his arms around me. I'd love to feel loved by him. Ah, what the heck! Wishing is for fairytales. The cold, hard reality is that he just couldn't be bothered. Just doesn't care about me. It's something I have got to accept.

If I reach high enough I can touch God. The mikes and cameras are working again. Click. Click. Click. All being transmitted to the world of death. Brainwaves being recorded by the Alien Force. I'm slowly being taken over. Dr. A is not a psychiatrist, she's one of them. I can't fight them anymore. And the other one! His shoulder patting — which of course is a cover up — has drained me of my life force, my energy. Well, it should keep him going for a few years yet. Soon I will be a zombie.

I don't want a disturbed psychiatrist! Saw Professor C and the doctor who says she's Dr. A and my student. I had to push them away from me this morning. They're not going to live off my life force — but I think it's too late, they have all they need to keep them going. Reality is here in this place. Unreality is outside. I think they have won. I am one of Them. I am another added to the multitude of the dead. Part dead, part alive — that's me. They haven't killed my body. It still functions. They've just killed my mind.

Imagine! This is a hospital. A psychiatric hospital. I have never seen so many disturbed doctors before. Who treats them? I'm a patient. Do we treat them when they have sessions with us? Do we sort out their confused disturbed minds at these doctor sessions? Do they know that they are patients as well?

I'm in reality. This mind of mine, full of confusion and fear and darkness is reality. This hospital is reality. How dare people say that it is not! How dare they say that I'm sick! That what I'm going through is not reality. Fools! Must I suffer them gladly? My mind IS reality — not sickness. Anyway, the only worthwhile things are drugs. They make me feel normal.

I'm out of that hospital. Have to come in every day for supervised medication. Scored palfium, devedrine and nembutal off Hairy Harry today. Wow, I really freaked out. Tried to break the windows on the bus. Was put off, naturally. Kept laughing at nothing. Everyone was staring at me. All I could do was laugh, laugh, laugh. Jumped onto the back of a motor bike at the traffic lights and tried to push the guy off. Was taken to the cop station. No charges.

Had my first fix in a month today. Speeding. Speeding. Speeding. I'm going to be killed. By whom? I don't know. Don't think. Withdraw. Knives, blades, grass — destroy myself. Laughing and I feel so sad. Oh, *shit* man, get another fix.

There's a seagull, no two seagulls in my bedroom just standing there staring at me. Two mute seagulls. A change from the usual screaming cries. Their eyes are huge and their beaks are covered in blood. I must have blacked out last night. The last thing I remember was the seagulls dripping blood and walking in slow motion towards me. That's all I remember.

Back in hospital. Jesus, I hate! There is so much hatred, anger and frightful unhappiness inside me. Cut my arms — thirty stitches — discharged myself from the hospital. Put my arms through a window — back in hospital for ten days — out, and cut myself with a carving knife — more stitches and blood drip.

God, I'm frightened. There are awful weird feelings in my head and body and they are becoming progressively worse. Then they lessen and then hit me again full blast. Sound is like quadraphonic. I feel that my mind, my whole being is being blown up. Just one shattering explosion. Man, this trip is a real bummer. Pure acid!

People I like — nobody. I'm a nobody. I have a body, but no mind. The Alien Beings are still using my mind.

Laughing — crying — laughing — crying — screaming — screaming — screaming —
SCREAMING
HELP ME
FOR CHRIST'S SAKE
SOMEBODY
HELP ME!!

Chapter 15

Gestalt

I attended gestalt therapy in St. Patrick's hospital, first as an in-patient, later as an out-patient. Gestalt means getting in touch with yourself. It means trying to stay in the here and now. It means becoming a whole. There's no confrontation with another person. You confront yourself.

You put a chair, with a cushion on it, in front of you and place yourself, your parents, drugs, sadness, aggression etc. in that chair. Then you get to a feeling level and you confront whatever or whoever you are feeling is "stopping your growth", bugging you. It's also a way of relieving aggression — instead of smashing a bottle or a window or smashing into yourself, you hit the cushion as hard as you can, keep hitting it, hitting it, harder, harder, harder, and, as you are smashing down on the cushion, pictures come into your mind.

Then the talking and screaming begin. "I *hate* you Dad! I *hate* life! I *hate* being a psychiatric patient!"

Then you have to switch to being "Dad", to being "life". It's like your mind clearing — you have to *be* Dad, drugs, hatred, all "talking back to you", and, after maybe an hour and a half, you find out *why* you're so full of aggression and hatred. It's emotionally exhausting, but after the sessions you feel calm and at peace.

This is how I started at one of these sessions. I put my depression on that cushion, and spoke to it as if it were a human being:

Lisa: Depression, you are black, cold and you are smothering me. Dragging me down. Making me a drag. You are giving me cravings for drugs — making me want to go back on them.

SWITCH: Be depression talking back

Depression: Yes. I'm black, cold and I *am* smothering you. Oh, I will get you back into the world of drugs again. I lost you to a kind of peace and happiness for some time, a *very short time*, my dear, very short! But now I have you back, and I'm not going to let you go! I will get you to the stage where you will be blinded, frozen, immobilised by me, back hard on drugs — oh, you will be so bad that you *will* kill yourself. There's nothing for you, no future — just drugs, groups and endless psychiatrists. Come on let me have you back — I want *all* of you.

SWITCH

Lisa: Oh, shut up! Shut up! Fuck off, will you ever fuck off! Sure, I'm taking diconal, palfium and Drinamyl, but not to the extent I was taking them, and I'm off the needle. You're horrible. Cold. So cold. And black. You're *frightening* me! Just go *away!* You're so damned strong! You're pulling me.

SWITCH

Depression: I won't go. You are far too weak to make me. A dirty, no-good junkie. Don't listen to those who say you are strong. It's easier to give in to me. I'm nice. I can also make you go back on drugs the way you were. The needle etc. Come on, you cowardly bitch, get right into me. Come on, depression is a *nice* feeling.

SWITCH

Lisa: I am not weak. I won't give in to you, pitiful depression. I won't go back on the needle for you. I won't sink back into hell again. I have let you get the better of me far too often. I *am* strong.

Very. It's you who are weak. I'm strong enough to say NO to you. I'm strong enough not to go back to the needle and hell. I'm strong enough to keep fighting the battle of trying to stay off gear. Of trying to stop sinking into "the black hole of Calcutta" which is you, you miserable depression. You won't get me back. You have made me so angry by calling me weak and a coward, that I *know* I can get the better of you . . . you ugly, cowardly depression, that's all you are. You suicide lover. Trapping people in your destructive grip. I'm a thousand times stronger than you. You are nothing — just a destructive weakling! You have made me so angry that I'm not depressed any more. I'm nice and warm inside — and strong! Oh, yes, another thing, I don't take those pills every day. Three times a week, maybe, but not every day like I used to.

SWITCH

Depression: It won't last, you know. It won't last. You make me sick!

SWITCH

Lisa: Each time you get hold of me, I will be that bit stronger to push you away. As for me making you sick — well, pitiful weakling, the feeling is mutual.

You make me feel like throwing up! Anyway, you fool, you are sick. Stupid idiot. I will never become one of your hopeless cases. Now, fuck off. I'm exhausted. I have you beaten and it's a good feeling. I feel on top of the world, not the world on top of me.

Chapter 16

From My Diary

It's amazing how tranquil one feels after talking in depth about one's feelings. I learnt something important at the centre tonight from a very good friend: Unless I like and accept myself I will always feel unwanted and rejected. I know I'm wanted, and should not be in a constant fear of being rejected, but because I don't really like myself — how can I like myself anyway, when I don't know myself, when my personality has never had a chance to develop? Because of my addiction, I think nobody wants or likes me. I wish I could break down the barriers. Fool! How can I break them down when I'm constantly in a haze of drugs?

I went through a "work out" on a feeling-level today. Feelings of hurt, despair, of anger and terror because I just can't kick the habit! I cried right from the very centre of my being. Not just from my mind, but from the empty hollow in my stomach. I feel I'm in the middle of a big storm — cry, cry, cry that storm to a sea of calmness.

Withdrawn. I'm hostile, aggressive. I hate people. Oh, God, why, why, why, did I ever take that first "barb" in school all those years ago. How in God's name could I know I would end up like this. I'm so tired. So tired emotionally and physically. I feel like an antiquated Alice in Wonderland, totally bewildered, confused. I'm becoming so vulnerable but it's to other people's suffering. My brain will not last out much longer. Neither will my body. I can't keep speeding day and night much longer. My emotions are fatigued. Everything seems so *tragic!* Oh, not only my mess — things like a dog in pain, a child crying. Things which would make me feel sad before. But, now, I've become over-sensitive to the suffering of others. I won't even read the paper or watch the news. My eyesight keeps going queer. Objects keep going blurred and appear to go into shadows. I'm having awful acid flashbacks. Sometimes when watching a film or someone talking their mouths move but emit no sound. I'm seeing huge spiders and flies crawling all over my skin, eating into my arm — got to keep it in my head, they're only acid flashbacks.

I wonder what it's like to be carefree and happy-go-lucky, but not drug-induced carefreeness? What it's like to be able to relax without popping pills to bring on a false relaxation? I wonder what that reality is like? Oh, God, if you love, please help me kick the habit!

Chapter 17

The Hypnotist

There is one thing that I remember very clearly from my stay in Dublin's psychiatric hospitals. It concerns an episode that is so incredible that many people will just say "she's telling lies again, like junkies always do." Or they'll say "it was just a hallucination, something that she dreamed when she was hypnotised. These things don't happen here." Okay, you judge it as you want to. I'll just tell it like I remember.

Medical students doing their finals have to do so many months of psychiatry and then do an exam in it — the same for doctors going on for psychiatry afterwards.

Patients are chosen for the doctors to do part of the exam, on "case histories". They ask all kinds of questions and then they make their diagnosis. I was chosen twice as the "guinea-pig".

The second time I was chosen, it was a young doctor that I had never seen before. The particular place I was in at the time had a men's ward and a female ward. The exams were normally held in the men's ward. But the doctor asked the head male nurse could he use one of the rooms, rather than ask me questions in the ward. Permission was granted.

He started off with the usual run-of-the-mill questions: age, date of birth, parents still alive, how many in the family, relationship between parents — good, bad, indifferent? (oh, spare me!) — and so on and so on and so on.

Then he said to me that I was very tense and could I try and relax. "Lie on top of the bed, and try and loosen up a bit. I'll draw the curtains, the darkness might help." Oh, God, I thought, not another of those ones who are into "back to the womb". So the questions went on, but now every second one came around to asking me about sex. Did I like it? Had I a boyfriend? Had I had sex? What was it like? Then the questions were just about sex. Nothing else. Just sex. Okay, that's alright in moderation — but not when it becomes highly personal, and when a detailed, step-by-step account is wanted!

Next: "Lisa, have you ever been under hypnosis?"

"No, doctor, I'm not a good subject for hypnosis." Which I wasn't.

"Well, I bet — in fact, I know — that I will be

able to get you under."

"But for what?"

"To relax you, of course, so that you can talk to me."

So I agreed — but I had no intention of letting myself be hypnotised, and I had no intention either of letting him know that I *wasn't* under hypnosis.

After a while, he asked me was I sleepy.

"Yes," I said, "very sleepy." Which I wasn't. Not one bit. I was aware of everything.

"I'm going to put you into a deeper state, Lisa."

A few minutes later, he was telling me "you are completely under my control, Lisa. I can make you do anything."

"Yes," I agreed, in a sleepy, dreamy voice, thinking to myself "like *hell* am I completely under your control. You couldn't get into the Gaiety Theatre with this miserable act! If you don't make it as a psychiatrist, you'll never make it as a hypnotist!"

What happened next was so amazing that I still can't believe, after all these years, that it actually did happen. The questions about sex — my views on sex, did I go the whole way, or did I enjoy heavy petting more — were literally becoming the sort of thing one would read in a pornographic magazine, and certainly of no benefit to him for forming a case history on me. No, just for getting sexually aroused — which, to my horror, he did. Twice I didn't answer some of his intimate, personal, detailed questions, but when I refused to answer he started to turn quite nasty, verbally. Now, according to him, I was under deep hypnosis, and would remember nothing when he'd bring me out of the hypnosis. By this stage I was too frightened of him to tell him that he hadn't succeeded in hypnotising me at all. Then he started touching me, saying "you like that, don't you?" — which I certainly didn't! He had moved over onto the bed and was sitting beside me. Slowly, he pulled up my jumper and started feeling my breasts, but he didn't undo my bra.

Next, his over-active wandering hands wandered down to the zip of my jeans. By this time I was rigid with fright. He unzipped my jeans, whispering all the time for me to relax, and he was just about to put his hand inside my jeans when there was a knock on the door.

Up went the zip. Back onto his chair went the doctor. A picture of total composure. Within me, a picture of total chaos. Disgust. Repulsion. Sheer panic. In came the head male nurse, and told the doctor his time was up. *His* time was up! Mine had just been on the verge of being up!

The doctor then proceeded to bring me out of my "deep hypnotic state", and slowly — very slowly — I pretended to "come out of the hypnosis". "What happened? Did I fall asleep?" Oh, total innocence!

The male nurse stayed until the doctor left the room. When he did leave, I was going to tell the nurse what had happened, but ... it would have been the patient's word against the doctor's. The nurse, actually, kept asking me was I all right? Did the doctor get permission to give me hypnosis? The nurse knew something had happened, I could see that, but I would tell him nothing. Apart from the fact that it would be my word against the doctor's, I was simply afraid of the doctor. Very afraid. Anyway, he would have said that it was just an hallucination under hypnosis, and proof that I was sexually disturbed!

I eventually managed to put the whole incident out of my mind. But about four months later, after I had been discharged from hospital, I was visiting a friend in hospital and who should I bump into but my "hypnotist", who was now in charge of the ward my friend was in. And he also used hypnosis on her frequently. I won't go into the sick, sordid details of what she told me about him. I knew her well. She never lied, never exaggerated. She only wanted one thing — to be cured of her drug addiction. That was the only thing she lied about: drugs, as all addicts do. I never went back to visit her again. Incidentally, she died two months later, a couple of weeks after being discharged, from an overdose of morphine. Afterwards, I heard that that doctor had left the hospital and given up medicine. God help the helplessness of patients put under the care of men like him.

Chapter 18

From My Diary

Man! I'm speeding and I can't stop. Must get in touch with Spacer and get something to bring me down. No! I won't. I'll get in touch with J —. Oh, wow, what a night! Now I'm fine. I'd been speeding night and day for ten days. Oh, Sleep, blessed Sleep. Ten days and no sleep — just speeding, speeding, sky high.

Went to see J —. The patience and gentleness of that man. He brought me through a beautiful fantasy (by telling me a sort of "lullaby story") of being in a boat. A small boat. Everything was so calm and beautiful. I actually went on that fantasy journey (in my mind) from Dun Laoghaire to Holyhead in a little cabin cruiser. It was a long, long journey. Very rough at first — we were tossed about something terrible. I thought we'd have to turn back, but we persevered, and very gradually the sea calmed down. When we were leaving Dun Laoghaire and out a good bit, all we could see were the lights of Dublin. It was like looking at one enormous, vast Christmas tree. The sky was an inky blue, dotted with stars, that reflected and sparkled on the water. There was one star that seemed to be with us all the time — as if guiding, protecting us.

The sea was calmer now. Not a sound except the chug-chug-chug of the engine, and the waves lapping off the side of the boat. In the distance there was a cold grey light breaking through the inky blackness above us. Into the light we sailed. It got brighter and became a warm glow of pink. What a long journey it had been. Rough and then calm. We were exhausted! Yet very relaxed and peaceful inside. We had made that long journey in that little boat, and had weathered the occasional storm, and had arrived safe.

I made that journey. I started that journey full of panic, of tension, my mind speeding a hundred miles an hour. I was exhausted, but I kept going, determined to reach "dry land". I sat at the helm keeping that boat on course during the storms. I thought the voyage was never going to end. At times I felt myself going off course, and then I could see the light of a new day breaking through the blackness, and I felt calm and peaceful. I had made that journey and had arrived safe. That star that was with me the whole journey — guiding, protecting was J —. J —, you helped me to help

myself last night. It was a tough journey at first —
but gradually became a beautiful, beautiful journey.
I didn't think I'd make it, but I did, and you were
with me all the time. You make me feel so safe,
and so secure. I feel wanted. A Fatherly love.

Chapter 19

Hooked on Heminevrin

For years, my anxiety and tension had run at a high pitch. I was unable to function unless I was doped up to the eyeballs with sedatives. I was unable to talk without stuttering and stammering, was always sweating and shaking with tension. My co-ordination would often go haywire. I used to feel as if I were either on a very bad trip or very, very drunk.

My first anxiety attack came when I was only eleven, before I ever *touched* drugs. No psychiatrist was able to cure me of the tension, the anxiety. No therapy. Oh, they got to the root cause — eventually — but the tension never left. Never eased. Drugs made it subside, of course — though they turned me practically into a vegetable — but the tension was always there, and surfaced when I was not on *anything*. The anxiety and tension were as sickening, as frightening, as horrible as withdrawals, and as dangerous as doing cold turkey.

When I got seriously into sedatives, as my main form of addiction, I didn't have to go to the pushers to get tranquillisers. There are enough GPs doing the same job as the pusher.

I never had any problem getting prescriptions. *Never.* One GP in particular knew I had had a hard drug problem, knew I had been in Coolemine, knew my whole case history, and after a couple of visits a month for valium must have known that I had become seriously addicted to it — yet he never once refused to give me a prescription. Always a six month script, and, as if that wasn't bad enough, I just had to spin his receptionist a story that I'd "lost" my prescription or my tablets, and I'd get another six-month prescription! How naive can you get? Doctors really need to be more clued in to the little ways of us drug addicts!

I usually had four or five scripts at once. Within a year I was going through a month's supply in ten days. Eighty-four valium; ten milligrams in ten days! Within two years I was taking 168 every week.

My doctor's pity for my tension and my anxiety nearly killed me. His sympathy for me over the fact that I had been in and out of hospitals for numerous operations, and his liking for me as a person, nearly killed me. I told him, loads of times, that I knew I was addicted and asked could I be taken gradually off the pills. He would do this for a few weeks. Then my cravings would get so bad that out of sheer terror I'd go back on hard gear, and because my mind and body so desperately needed something, I'd go back to him, and I'd be back to square one.

I tried everything I could think of to help me to come off them, and to be able to relax naturally, to go through the tensions and anxieties everyone goes through, but not that sky-high anxiety and tension. Nothing worked, though. So I gave up trying and surrendered to a year and a half of total addiction to valium. In its own way, it's nearly as bad as a hard drug addiction.

* * *

Some years ago I had to go into hospital for four months for an operation. I brought massive doses of valium in with me (hidden of course), along with my repeat prescriptions. I also brought a hard drug I had been scoring off one of my old suppliers. I had roughly fifty tabs of this drug with me, as well as four large bottles of valium. After about three months, I ran out of the valium, and I had gone through the other tabs in the first six weeks. One of the cleaners then went to different chemists with the prescriptions for valium for me, on condition that I gave her quite a lot of money. I also used to save up the painkillers I was on, and would take them when I had enough to dope me.

I hated what I was doing. I hated myself. Despised myself ... but, I couldn't stop. I couldn't *help* it.

Then, two weeks before Christmas I told the cleaner to get to hell, not to get me any more tablets, and that if she reported me to the sister of the ward, I would report her to the matron, to the cleaners' supervisor, to my doctor, and tell them the amount of money I had had to give her, along with the money for the prescriptions. I tore up the prescriptions and made up my mind to sweat it out. I wasn't so scared of fits since I was in a hospital.

Jesus Christ! I stuck it out until Stephen's Day — I thought I was going to die. I got the doctor on duty and told him I seemed to be having some sort of breakdown and that it seemed to be taking the form of severe withdrawals — even then I couldn't bring myself to tell the truth. Now, that hospital is an excellent one, and had my complete case history. Hard drug addict, and so on — the lot. My psychiatrist had been coming in once a week to see me. They knew I was under psychiatric care.

One of the staff rang my old hospital, and spoke to somebody there (it was night time). I don't know if my case history was given. All I know is that a terrible mistake was made. It was partly my fault, because I didn't say I *was* going through withdrawals, but, most certainly, it was only *partly* my fault.

The tablets that were prescribed for me were called Heminevrin. These are given to alcoholics for withdrawals, and in some cases to old people. But to give them to someone who had had a severe drug problem, a long history of drug abuse was sheer madness, and a terrible lack of communication between people who had been dealing with me, not to mention total failure on the part of the medical profession generally, not just for putting me on them, but because I was never taken off them. The dosage was never reduced, and I was sent home six and a half weeks later on a month's prescription.

I'd never seen those capsules before they gave them to me in that hospital. For a week they knocked me out cold — then, they began to lose their effect, and I noticed that they made me feel very relaxed, and gave me a feeling of well being. Within ten days I knew what was happening. I was slowly, very slowly, becoming dependent on them.

I started saving them up in hospital, and I'd take three together. The effects would last only two hours though and when they wore off I felt lousy and just counted the hours until the medication was given out again. I then counted more hours until I had enough saved up to satisfy my mind and at this stage (though I didn't know it) my body. I thought I had become psychologically dependent on Heminevrin tablets, because they made me feel so relaxed. I didn't know I had also become physically dependent on them.

I didn't know that they were highly addictive and frightfully dangerous. That, taken in excess — the way I was eventually to take them — they could cause brain damage, blackouts, impairment of memory, fits, and even death if withdrawals aren't supervised — if one were suddenly to stop taking them. Heminevrin tablets have long-lasting serious effects, and can do as much damage as barbs, speed or cocaine. They are just as hard to get off and stay off, if one becomes addicted.

I was yet to find all that out! Jesus Christ! Doctors! Where's their cop-on, their sense of responsibility, their duty, their care? Not all doctors of course, but, my God, a hell of a lot of them!

When I was sixteen I was put on a lotion for acne. I was on that lotion for seven years until, two years ago, a chemist told me to be very careful over the amount I was using. I used to put lashings of it on. The chemist told me that it contained cortisone which can cause excessive hair growth on the face. I checked this out and found it to be true. One doctor who gave me prescriptions for valium had me on that lotion for two years, without warning me of the harm it can do, if used too much and too long.

When I left the hospital I asked the doctor for a script for Heminevrin, which I got. Two weeks later I went up to the ward I had been in, saw the house doctor, and asked him for another prescription, which I got. I then went up to my GP, said I had had a breakdown in the hospital, described the tablets they had given me — pretending I didn't know the name of the capsules — and got a six month Heminevrin prescription from him, as well as a six month prescription for valium.

I brought the prescription to a new chemist near where my flat was. The other chemist on that road had never, never taken my script for valium. I hated him for that. Now I have the deepest respect for him. He knew I had a problem. How he was able to tell, *I* don't know, but he knew.

Anyway, the new chemist simply oozed charm. He took my script and gave me the caps and valium. That prescription was a repeat script, but the chemist said he would keep it, and anytime I wanted the caps and valium just to come up to him and he'd never see me short.

This was great! I could hardly believe it. Manna from heaven! Within two weeks I was back to him. He asked me how many I wanted, *never* mentioning the fact that he had given me a month's supply of each only two weeks previously. I got thirty caps and thirty valium. After six weeks I was going to him every seven to ten days and getting either forty-two or twenty-eight caps — sometimes even sixty — together with the valium. This went on until March. By then I knew I had a serious problem with the Heminevrin, but I *still* didn't know just *how* serious.

I was getting scared. I couldn't get back my prescription from the chemist. I wanted to stop those drugs — to reduce them gradually. I sent two friends up to the chemist, who told him I was going home for a while (which was true) and I needed my prescription. I could hardly believe it when I saw the prescription. I knew why he had been so reluctant to hand it over. He had written down false dates and wrong amounts on it. Now I had kept a diary of the dates and of the amounts that had been dispensed. He hadn't once stamped the prescription when he had been dispensing the caps and tablets, and obviously had not entered them into a book as all chemists are supposed to do.

I went home and cut myself down very slowly. Then only three days later I went rigid with tension, got frightful cravings — the usual. So, I went up to my GP and got another prescription. Back to the old routine. I now had two scripts for Heminevrin. I got 180 between the two, and 164 valium. I stayed at home for ten days, making life hell for my family. Then I went back to the flat, rang my GP and told him I'd lost the prescription. He said he would send another script in the post. I now had *three* prescriptions. I found another GP who informed me that Heminevrin were harmless. He gave me another six month prescription. Now I had *four* prescriptions and a new chemist! *This* chemist used to give me valium even if I didn't have a prescription. And so I went to him with the prescriptions for the Hem and valium, as *well* as to my kindly, charm-oozing chemist down the road. Between the four scripts I could now get 398 Hem and 280 valium a month.

After a few months the majority of chemists noticed that I had a problem, and refused to dispense the drugs to me. But, there's always a small minority who will dispense anything — even suspecting that they are handing out stuff to people with a drug problem — be it hard drugs or soft drugs, tranquillisers or sleeping pills. It's the same with GPs. There is always a handful who will hand out practically anything you ask them for — even if you have a drug problem. When you attend a doctor for some time and keep asking for scripts, well, they *must* know the situation after a while. But, as I found out, they just turn a blind eye. Or maybe they think it's my own responsibility.

By now I was having blackouts, my co-ordination kept going haywire. I was passing out in buses, in cafés. I'd close my eyes, and go into a very deep sleep. I suppose it was a sort of overdose due to the massive dosage I was now taking. I was making life miserable for my family — the worry, the helplessness, the unhappiness, the hell I was putting them through, the hell that was so familiar. The hell they thought would never descend on them again since I went off hard drugs.

One day I read an article on The Rutland Centre. I was struck by the success rate they have. I rang Rutland and made an appointment with one of the counsellors. A week later I saw her. She was down-to-earth, took no bull, could be brutal — for one's own good — and, as I was to find out many months later, she has a heart of gold and is a genuine caring person beneath a tough exterior.

She rang Jervis Street, and made an appointment

for me. A week later I saw the doctor in the drug clinic. He wanted to take me in within a day or two. I wanted to attend as an outpatient. This we agreed on. I was to come in seven days a week for medication — to be reduced very slowly over the weeks.

In ten days I was off valium. For the first four weeks I did fine on the reduction of the Hem, then when it got down to eight a day, I got a script from my GP — without telling the doctor in the clinic of course. Within a few days I was taking twelve a day, *plus* the eight I got from the clinic. As my medication was reduced further, my intake of Hem increased. Soon I was taking thirty a day. Then my medication from the clinic was finished, except for tablets to prevent withdrawal fits, and the doctor wanted me to go into the detoxification unit for a few days before going to the Rutland Centre. I went in. I was fine the first two days, then the sweating, shaking and vomiting started, so I had to tell the doctor what I had been doing. I was put back on medication. I was also a wreck from tension and anxiety. So I was kept in hospital for six weeks. Within the six weeks I was assessed for Rutland, and it was decided that I wouldn't be able for the intensity of the programme. It wouldn't have been fair on me. To quote the counsellor, "it would be just another failure to add to my already long list of failures," which was sound and right on.

The week before I left the detox, the social

workers started up a group meeting once a week for patients like me. It was a good group. No heavy confrontations. Plain, truthful talking. Relating to one another. Giving support to one another. Helping each other.

The day I left the detox, I survived one hour! In the unit, you are in a nine-bedded ward. You have no situations, no confrontations — it's sort of like being in a cocoon. A womb.

It's pretty mind blowing, after six weeks, to be pulled out of the womb. Reality is softened in *any* hospital: the noise of the traffic; the amount of people. Reality. Okay, I tell myself I could have taken it *if* I were not fraught with tension and anxiety. Even after six weeks I was still sweating, choking, stammering. I tried to get down to the shops — three minutes walk — but I could not get out the door of my flat. History repeating itself — exactly the way I felt after coming off hard gear. I know it sounds crazy, but I could not do ordinary things. I was too tense.

Anyway, I got a friend to bring my script to the chemist (six month repeat). I threw away all the valium, but not the Hem. It would have been a hell of a lot better if I'd thrown away all the Hem and not the valium. Within four days of leaving Jervis Street, I was taking ten caps. Not all together — but I'd go throughout ten during the day. I'd been dried out for five weeks. I had no tolerance. One day I went through the ten caps, fell asleep on the bed, and my flatmates couldn't wake me. When I did wake up I was in the recovery ward in the Meath. I'd had a wash-out while I was still in that deep sleep. It wasn't a coma. I wasn't unconscious. I just went into a very, very, deep sleep. It was, I suppose, an overdose.

As soon as I got out of the hospital, I went back to my charming chemist. He's not worthy of being called a chemist, of having those letters after his name. Such an idiot, so gullible. Spun him a yarn about having mislaid my tablets, and got ninety-two capsules. On the same day I rang my GP and asked him for a script. I told him I'd been down the country and had lost my prescription and the tablets. No questions were asked — I got the prescription in the post two days later. My mother had told this doctor that I had become badly addicted to Heminevrin, and that I'd been addicted to valium. She explained to him that I had gone onto tranquillisers after coming off hard gear and had first become addicted to valium and then Hem. He knew I'd just come out of Jervis Street. She had also asked him *never* to give me a script for Hem or valium again, no matter what story I told him. Yet he did. And continued to do so. And his partner also gave me scripts. Sometimes, only a week after my doctor would post out a script to me, I'd ring his partner and get another script. Always a six month repeat prescription, and in the two years I was getting them, they were never *once* reduced. Many a time those doctors would actually ask me: "How many a day, Lisa, is it four a day or three?"

"Have I got you on them at night now, as well as during the day?" When I think about that I get so angry, and so terribly depressed. I put all the blame on the doctors. Yet it's my own fault too, for fooling them and spinning them yarns, when they're too busy to check out all the details of my medication.

I was supposed to attend the clinic to see the social worker, and give a urine sample, and attend the group. I attended the social worker for a while, then started to cancel appointments because I knew the Hem would show up in the urine sample, and because I was so spaced out that it was impossible for me to go and talk to her. I attended only four group sessions.

Eventually I stopped going to the clinic altogether. I was back to square one. I had no control over my life. Heminevrin controlled it. By now I was going through thirty to thirty-six a day. I made life a living hell for my two flatmates and for three other friends who were to stand by me throughout the two years. I was having frequent blackouts, my speech was slurred, half the time I didn't know what I was doing, I'd have memory losses for four or five hours. I fell asleep smoking loads of times. My friends would often find me in that peculiar deep sleep, on the floor, on the bed, in the kitchen. They could never wake me up — I'd wake up myself eventually, in bed. I might have been on the phone, or eating my tea, or watching TV, and the next thing it would be morning or night and I'd be in bed, having passed out wherever I'd been or whatever I'd been doing. By now I was never short of a script for Hem. I ran out of the caps only three times, and had to wait until the physical withdrawals had eased, then get the GP to post me a script, or make it to the chemist to get more.

Chapter 20

Trying to Escape

If it weren't for the support of my five friends, I'd have gone back on hard gear or killed myself. No way were they soft on me — quite the opposite. At times I hated them for the things they said to me, but everything they said about my behaviour was true.

They weren't afraid to tell me the hard, harsh truth. They weren't afraid to hurt me. They *cared* about me.

Six weeks after I had been discharged from hospital I asked another doctor to take me in for a few days to dry me out yet again — which he did. Three days after I had been admitted, I went into a desperate state of paranoia. I overheard remarks concerning myself which I should never, never have heard and this contributed to the state I got into. My one consolation — and to this day I still laugh

over it — was that there was another patient I had
got friendly with. One night I went into her room
in tears saying: "God, I can't stick it, those nurses
are talking about me non-stop! Twenty-four hours
a day!" At which she looked at me in genuine
amazement and replied "But, Lisa, how can they
possibly be talking about *you* all the time, when
they're talking about *me*? They haven't stopped
talking about me since I was admitted!"

So I finally worked it out that they divided up
their time talking about us. They talked about me
for twelve hours, and for the other twelve they
talked about her. We split our paranoia in two.
Poor consolation!

Five days after I was admitted I discharged
myself. For a number of reasons. I couldn't recover
from my paranoia. The conversation and remarks I
had overheard had upset me, more than I was ever
to let anyone know, with the result that the
confidence and trust I'd had in the staff turned to
distrust and bitterness.

I was still going through withdrawals when I left.
Naturally, I was not allowed out on medication,
except tablets to prevent withdrawal fits. The day I
discharged myself I was so bad with tension that
my muscles stiffened up and I was unable to write
my name on the discharge form. A nurse had to
hold the pen and my hand and help me. I've seen
patients come in like that, but *very* few leave that
way. I got a taxi home, and for five days I couldn't
walk — I was rigid with tension — I was also still

going through withdrawal. I stayed at home with my family for five weeks, sky high with tension and anxiety. I was taking nothing. I really thought I'd make it ... this time.

But once again I was in a cocoon of security. All I had to do was watch TV and play with the dog. Oh, I cooked my own meals, and talked to my family as best I could. *That* was hard. I felt so weird inside that I thought it showed, and so I mostly kept to myself.

Then I decided to go back to the flat, thinking — well, I will try again. I really meant it. The very next day I went to the shops and was unable to ask for what I wanted. I was unable to answer the phone, the door, I couldn't get on a bus, I couldn't go to the bank to cash my cheques.

I stuck it out for a week, then rang my GP and ... the six month script arrived in the post two days later.

A week later, I rang his partner, spun the usual story; two days later a six month repeat script arrived in the post.

Same day went to a GP who used to give me a lot of valium, spun a story to him and got a six month repeat script. I had three scripts by now and didn't have to bring any prescription to that nice chemist of mine — just had to ask him for thirty days supply and got them.

The next few months are hazy. I was taking forty a day by January. By September I was taking sixty-two. I'd be able to stay off them for a few days because I had so much in my system, but as soon as the withdrawals started I'd go back on them again. I was becoming nearly as bad as I had been on hard drugs. It was like a repetition of the years of hard drug abuse. It got to the stage at which I would really believe that I hadn't taken anything when confronted by my friends. They'd scream at me that I had taken something and to stop lying, and I'd scream back at them that I hadn't taken a thing, and I really believed I hadn't.

By now, most of the chemists had caught on to me — but a lot hadn't — well, if they had, they still gave the drugs to me. So I used to do a tour of the chemists every five days, or every two weeks, leaving in prescriptions and in the case of one chemist, just getting the capsules without a script. He knew me well at this stage. How he could have given them to me still is beyond my comprehension, as I used to stagger, reel in to him, talk as if I were sloshed out of my mind on drink, and stagger out again. I was often tempted to get a can of spray paint, go down to his chemist some night, and paint on the door and window "The Stagger Inn". (At the pub up the road, they stagger out at closing time, here you stagger in).

One day I read an article on an acupuncturist. I took down his address, wrote to him, telling him *everything* about myself. Two days later I got a really encouraging letter from him, asking me to write to him again for an appointment for a consultation. I went down — his practice is in the country

— a week later. I stayed with friends, who drove me out to him. He was willing to take me on if I could find a place to stay nearby. As that was impossible he tried to arrange it that I would be admitted to hospital down there, but that fell through. He finally referred me to a doctor here in Dublin who also does acupuncture. I didn't bother ringing this doctor however, as I just felt "oh, God, what's the use?"

Then I began to go over things in my mind. Finally, I decided to ring him, explain everything, stressing the fact that when I was dried out even after two months I couldn't function because of tension and anxiety, and that this was nearly killing me. I craved normal tension, normal anxiety. I craved being able to relax. Oh, of course, I still craved Hem most of all, and my addiction hadn't lessened. But from past experience I knew that there were two cravings — first for the drugs, then, when I was dried out, a craving for relaxation and normality. It was usually this second need that sent me back to the drugs. I decided that I would tell this doctor that I particularly wanted acupuncture for severe tension and anxiety, telling him also about my addiction, the whole lot. I knew I would have to go through withdrawals again, but if the acupuncture worked for the tension and anxiety, then life would be so much, oh so much easier to live.

The whole thing was having a terrible affect on one of my flatmates in particular, and for her sake as well as my own I started to reduce very slowly. After two and a half weeks I started withdrawals. I didn't tell anyone, though I was terrified I'd take a withdrawal fit.

Withdrawals usually vary in time. These ones lasted five and a half days after I had reduced myself very slowly from forty down to nothing. Then for ten and a half days I took absolutely nothing, and the tension and anxiety were mounting each day. On the tenth day I had an awful feeling I was going to die or have a stroke from tension. I knew something was going to happen. What did happen was *horrific, terrifying!* I was watching TV, then went down to the kitchen, washed some dishes, and then went to bed. Next thing I knew there were two ambulance men, one of the girls in my flat and two girls from the flat above us, in the room. My flatmate had heard me choking and found me rigid on the bed and blue in the face.

I was brought to St. James's and given oxygen. I kept screaming "oh, God, I'm dying! Please, oh please, don't let me die!" — over and over again.

I knew something terrible was happening to me completely out of the ordinary. Then I started vomiting and didn't stop until about three in the morning. I wasn't able to tell the casualty doctor what was wrong with me, as I hadn't a clue what had happened. All I could do was groan, beg them not to let me die, and vomit. The casualty officer examined my stomach and pronounced: "A classic case of gastro enteritis." He told me I'd be fine, and that I could go home in the morning.

I went back to the flat in the morning, with nothing on me except a nightdress, a dressing gown and a pair of socks. Got into bed, felt I was going to be sick again, so I got out, put my head between my knees. The sickness passed. Went up to the front room, sat down beside my flatmate and tried to concentrate on the TV. Next thing I knew the room seemed to be full of people, the same people that had been in my bedroom the previous night — two ambulance men, flatmate and two girls from upstairs. This time I didn't recognise any of the girls. I hadn't a clue who they were. When I came back to the flat six weeks later one of the girls told me exactly what had happened. I had suddenly gone rigid and blue in the face again. I couldn't breathe properly as the muscles in my neck and face had stiffened up. My legs and body were jerking a lot. One of the girls was going to do artificial respiration as I seemed to have stopped breathing altogether but she decided not to as I was too rigid with tension. Apparently my eyes were open all the time.

I remember being in the ambulance. Getting oxygen again and vomiting violently. Again I wasn't able to tell the doctors anything. I couldn't understand why they kept looking at my eyelids and asking me did I always have blue eyelids. All I could do was vomit, vomit and vomit. They'd get part of my body relaxed, but as soon as they'd start on another part, the part they had relaxed

would stiffen up again. Luckily, the girls had rung
my mother and told her what had happened, so she
arrived soon after I had been brought in, and was
able to tell the doctors my case history of drug
abuse and operations, the lot. She knew also that
I'd been on nothing for eleven days.

I couldn't understand why my mother was looking so worried. I couldn't stop talking — when I
wasn't vomiting — I hadn't a clue why I was in
hospital again — I didn't even question it, not even
when I was admitted and brought up to the ward. I
still felt awful, but the horrific experience that I
was to go through for seven days had yet to come,
and it started early the next morning.

What I went through will haunt me for the rest
of my life, it was so terrifying — but worse, so real.
Oh, God, so very, very real.

*I fell asleep soon after being brought up to the
ward. When I woke up I thought — no, not thought
— believed I had gone back in time, way back
before civilisation. I had gone back to the ape man.
I knew I was in a hospital, but I couldn't understand
why the nurses and the other five patients looked
like apes. Naturally, I got hysterical and one of the
nurses came over to me. I couldn't look at her. She
— they all — had oversized heads, thick lips, long
arms, and were covered in hair. But when she
spoke to me, I couldn't understand what she was
saying, she seemed to be talking in another
language. When the doctor came, he too looked
like an ape and again I couldn't understand what*

138

he was saying. It wasn't English — it was like pre-historic language. I don't know how pre-historic man talked, but this sounded like how they would have spoken. I was put on a drip, and I thought they were trying to bring me back to 1981 by some sort of substance in the drip.

Worse was to follow as the hours went by. I had it figured out that there had been a nuclear war and civilisation had been wiped out. I believed, really believed, that I had died and was born again, but that I had been born way back before civilisation, and that this was the beginning of a new world. Evolution was to start again.

I also believed that God had shown me hell and was going to leave me in it for a while. The weirdest thing was that when I lay on my right side, with my head pressed down, everyone looked like an ape and I felt *I* was the one human being there, but when I lay on the left side, *I* was the ape and I could see everyone else as human. When I lay on my right side I couldn't understand a *word* anyone was saying. But when I lay on my left side, I could understand what they were saying, and, as I thought, was able to carry on a conversation with the staff. What I didn't know was that I was talking gibberish to them! The doctors told my parents this, and I wasn't told until I had been sent home again. I had understood what I was saying, but all the time I had been talking gibberish.

When I lay on my back, the right side and left side would sort of fuse and everyone would look half human, half ape. But I couldn't stay on my back trying to figure out which was the normal side — ape or human? And so I would change to my left, back to my right, twist and turn, twist and turn. As a result the drip kept coming out. The awful thing was that instead of getting better, I was becoming progressively worse. I kept saying: "Well, it can't get any worse — it's got to get better in a while — He's got to let me out of hell." Then I came out of hell, and I met this person, and I knew him and he knew me. He looked normal to me and I could understand what he was saying and he could understand me. So I stopped talking to the staff — the apes, the half humans — and would talk only to this person. I thought he was God, but he wasn't called God, he was called Og. I kept trying to say God, but I couldn't, only Og. Never once did I feel afraid with him.

But the horror I was seeing in the ward never subsided. I think one night I wouldn't stop screaming. I remember asking this person "Og" to please take me out of the horror — that I had been punished enough for my sins and now I wanted to see a miracle. I kept promising to be good — and that, yes, Og, I promise, I will spread the word through this new world that you *do* exist. And so does your son. I kept screaming: "Any time now, very soon, I'm going to die again and then I will be alright." I kept shouting: "Is this it? Have I died yet? Is this how I should feel, Og?" I'd go on my right side and call out: "Is this it then, is this the way everyone feels?" Then I'd say to myself: "No, it couldn't be, I'll go on my left side." And I'd go on my left side and repeat the question.

A psychiatrist was called in and he put me on little white tablets, but they didn't work, didn't do a thing for me. They were probably placebos. My parents had been told I was going to St. Patrick's but when my mother rang up the psychiatrist I had been attending, he said that it would be a step backwards. She practically begged him to take me in, to help me. But, no.

I don't think he can have known that I was so sick. It seemed to me like a lack of communication between doctors and between hospitals.

The hospital discharged me on the understanding that I would be going to St. Patrick's the next day.

I remember leaving that hospital. I will never forget it. My mother and father came in for me. One of the nurses dressed me — I couldn't even do that. When I was sitting on the side of the bed, everyone looked normal and I didn't feel that I was an ape either. Then suddenly my legs started jerking, going faster and faster, and then my whole body kept going into one massive jerk, would stop, and then jerk again — my legs jerking continuously. Two of the nurses tried to do something to stop the jerking, but I kept crying for my mother. Eventually they brought her into the ward. I knew her. I knew she was my mother. She kept saying to me: "It's alright, it's only tension; you're alright, it's just tension." And I kept saying over and over again: "Tension, it's just tension, I'm alright, it's just tension." My legs stopped jerking after a while, and my body stopped going into massive jerks.

When we were waiting for the lift a patient went by on an operating trolley, and I said to my mother: "But, he's a human! He's not an ape, he's a human being!" For the previous week I had seen a constant stream of apes being brought down to the theatre.

When we were driving home (I don't remember this, my parents told me a few days later) I started jerking violently and talking gibberish again. I kept saying: "Ride with the tension. Daddy, will I be alright, if I go along with the tension?" — and then laughing hysterically. The jerking, the hysterical laughter and the gibberish talk continued at home. When they managed to get me to bed, the horror I experienced in the hospital started again. I hadn't a clue who my mother, father, sisters were. I asked: "Who is that woman? I don't like her." That woman was my mother! Dad kept coming into the bedroom — but I didn't know who he was, except that my sisters called him by the name "Daddy". Oh, wow, talk about being on the brink of insanity! I remember shouting over and over again: "Og, where are you? Where are you, Og? Oh, please come back, please come back."

Then, suddenly, everything I had experienced in the hospital hit me full blast and I could feel myself falling, falling, falling into blackness. I could hear someone screaming. I kept shouting to whoever was screaming to stop! "Stop screaming!" But the screaming went on and on. The man called "Daddy", and a woman, and two girls, were in my bedroom. The man and woman were holding me. Then the screaming, that awful screaming, full of terror, stopped, my head cleared and the seven days of horror went. I recognised Mammy, Daddy and my two sisters — everything. That terrifying screaming was my screaming.

For five weeks I stayed at home, venturing out only as far as the garden. I still shook and sweated a lot for five whole weeks. Then I decided to go back to the flat. I was a wreck from tension. Again, I couldn't go to the shops, answer the phone. I just wanted to stay hidden in my bedroom all the time, and so ... rang my GP, got a prescription (six month repeat) and within two weeks had worked my way right back up to thirty-six a day. I also got a script from his partner.

My mother had rung up the acupuncturist I had been referred to and I was to see him in January. I tried, I really tried to hold out, but I just was not able.

So each day I increased the dosage. By the beginning of January I was taking sixty-two a day.

The second week in January I went to see the acupuncturist — he knew all about my drug problem, my severe anxiety, my tension. I had my first treatment that day. My tablets were reduced to eight a day. In two weeks I had three treatments and by the second week I was reduced to six Hem a day. Sure, I went through withdrawals, but they were *mild!* I could *cope!* Each time I feel an attack of anxiety and tension coming on I just rub the pins and the attack subsides. It's now the second week in March, as I write these lines, and I'm on two Heminevrin a day. I will have to have acupuncture until about October. Now, I only have it once a month. I can *cope* with everyday living. I can actually *cope* with the things that used to immobilise me. *I'm living! My mind is clear. I'm alive!* Oh, it's by *no* means easy. It's very, very hard.

Publisher's Note: Just how hard it is becomes clear on reading Chapter 24, "Another Setback", which takes up the story of Lisa's struggles with Heminevrin later that same year.

Chapter 21

Flashback

Looking back over the years, who am I now, what have I done with my life?

I'm a drug addict. I started dropping barbiturates at twelve. By the time I was thirteen I was into the whole "barb family"; I was into amphetamines, acid, and smoking hash. At thirteen I was addicted. At fourteen I was dropping as much acid as I could get, plus Mandrax, Cocaine, Codeine. By then I had an everyday habit.

Three days after my fifteenth birthday I started skin popping. Then, six months later, injecting into the veins. Then I became hooked on Pethidine, Methadone, Morphine and Physeptone (which were given to me to bring me down from hard drugs). It seems everything I took developed a habit — and a bad one.

Then I started taking valium, initially ten tablets

a day working my way up to ninety on top of everything else. Then cough bottles. Later I started snorting heroin, then fixing hard drugs, but it usually remained a weekend habit — I was lucky.

When I first got into the scene, as a young kid, before my addiction *really* set in, I thought I was the greatest. Hanging around Stephen's Green with guys and girls *years* older than me, wearing outrageous hippy clothes, flowers in our hair, patches on our jeans that said "Love and Peace", tee-shirts with "Peace" printed on the front and "Love and Happiness" on the back. Oh, yeah, the great spaced-out junkie image. Junkie! I wasn't even a real junkie then. But I loved the whole image. Flowers, love and peace. The guys strumming their guitars, a faraway expression on their faces, raggy jeans, Afro hairstyles, colours in the hair, outlandish make-up, the more way out the better. Dirty fingernails. Sitting around stoned, laughing at the straights, with their nine-to-five jobs and lives full of hassle. Reality! What a downer!

But then, when the addiction really set in, the Stephen's Green trip went bad, the "junkie pubs" held no more for me. The so-called fun and so-called appeal went down into a dark tunnel of sheer hell. Oh, how I longed to be one of the straights we had laughed at. But drugs held me in their grip, and I just lived from day to day for my supply of pills, and later for my fix. I had entered the living death of the junkie's world.

Before I started taking off from home, I had

become impossible to live with. I was rude, aggressive, hysterical, violent, anti-social, and had my parents on the verge of breakdown. I was full of hatred for my family, with no justification. I was selfish. A really horrible bitch.

I used to get into frightful rages and would wreck my bedroom — tearing pictures, smashing things, flinging the bedclothes all over the room. It was chaos. Every evening there would be a frightful row. My father shouting, my mother shouting, my sister crying, my other sister withdrawing quietly into herself, finally my mother breaking down and crying — and I'd just keep on screaming and shouting and hurling the most awful abuse at them.

Nine times out of ten I would start those terrible rows deliberately. Drugs had begun to eat into my personality, and the rot was steadily setting in. I had become unbearable. It had a frightful effect on my whole family. There was tension you could cut with a knife.

It's only in the last twelve months that my sister has been able to have real conversations with me. Her dislike for me has gone, as has my hostility, and that's made me very happy. Now I can relax with Dad too, talk to him, laugh with him, share the same interests.

At first, it was great crashing in on other people's pads, as long as I had a home to go to whenever I wanted. But then I got so bad I couldn't go home — so I left altogether. For years I slept rough on the streets, squatted, slept in derelict houses, rummaged through dustbins to see if there was anything "decent" to eat, lived in hovels that were called bedsitters. I became a complete dropout, and my standards went down to nothing.

As well as shoplifting — years of it, hundreds of pounds a week — I was into prostitution for a year and a half, to keep my habit going. I went to live in a commune full of freaks. I got into dealing in drugs here and in England, broke into chemists, doctors' surgeries, hospitals. I was busted numerous times; the courts always sent me to Brendan's for the "cure" — to no avail. I mixed with weird people. One junkie I knew had even killed a guy in England, when he had no money for drugs. This guy had previously ripped him off, so he did the same to him. Only he gave him a "hot shot" and left him dead. He got his supply, though — four days of morphine and acid.

It was around this time that myself and another guy — I was going out with him at the time — decided to set up our own "shooting gallery", for the heroin addicts to inject their drugs. We had all the proper equipment: syringes, needles, tourniquets (belts, actually) — and of course the heroin itself. This was done from the guy's flat. He used to charge an astronomical fee, and he always made sure we'd get our money first. When the junkies had had their shot, they used to space out, and then go on the nod. Then they would take themselves off somewhere, and come back for another fix.

With the money coming into the flat, we were never short of drugs. Also, we had no agonising mind hassles over where to look for cash. Which was great, because shoplifting wasn't on any longer for us. The big stores in Dublin knew our methods by now, and we were usually in a pretty bad state, so we looked too conspicuous.

Then, our three months of heaven finally ended. The guy got tipped off that his pad was going to be raided. The squad had had their eye on the place for a while. So we cleaned out the flat of all the evidence, sold the syringes, the needles and the heroin to the addicts, spent all the money between us, and then he went off to England, and later to America. I never heard from him again.

So it was back to forging scripts, stealing from doctors and hospitals, breaking and entering, and going on jaunts down the country to shoplift. I moved back into the commune again, where I had lived before, and one of the guys there had a van, so we used to go off down the country in that van, and go around the stores in a country town, ripping things off, and head back to Dublin with the van loaded with stolen goods.

And so it went on. I have been through cold turkey numerous times, spent the night in the cells of police stations more times than I care to remember, over-dosed accidentally nine times, was detoxified twelve times — but I never really wanted to come off drugs. Then, I was too terrified to live a drug-free life. I *hated* being a junkie, but I was too frightened to come off gear.

I had a feeling I was going to die soon, but it didn't bother me. I wanted to — I had reached gutter level. I could feel nothing when I heard that five of my friends were dead and one had the mind of a three-year old, in a twenty-six year old body, and was paralysed from the waist down — the very girl who showed me how to fix, a hundred years ago. I could feel nothing. I had no emotions, except to get my next fix or pill. I got two girls and two boys to push for me, as well as doing my own pushing. I guess I started those four off on drugs, but I had to do it to keep *my* habit going. Sometimes I'd give them drugs, mostly money — stolen of course. Very few drug addicts make it. Most end up in the morgue, or spend the rest of their days in a psychiatric hospital.

By now I had only three veins left and after the initial effect of what I fixed or popped had worn off — at this stage I had to have something every hour or two hours — I just wanted to lie down and die. One afternoon I went into a field, took three bottles of barbs and woke up two days later in the Meath. The doctors don't know how I made it. They had told my parents that it was out of their hands, they had done all they could, and it was in God's hands.

Oh, Mammy, Dad and my sisters — what heartache, heartbreak, what suffering I put you through. I didn't want to live. I wasn't grateful I was alive. And three more overdoses followed after that. I had no friends — addicts or straights. I was a filthy, smelly walking zombie. Drugs were just making me sick, sick, sick, but I couldn't get off them. I used to sit in a church and cry; for myself, my family. I was beginning to feel one emotion only — sadness.

I was having terrible black-outs. I would be in a shop and next thing I'd find myself on the beach. Hours would have gone by but I never had *any* recollection how I would have got from one place to the other. This happened more and more frequently.

All I did all day was scoring and then sitting in the park or in a derelict house. Scoring, scoring, scoring. Pushing. Then back to the park or house. Or just walking aimlessly around Dublin, well aware that everyone was staring at me. I never wore shoes. My jeans were frayed at the end, and my white smock was torn and filthy. The jeans were falling off me as I had gone down from nine stone six to seven stone four. I looked like something out of Belsen. I remember three women and two men came up to me and pressed money into my hand and said "Here dearie, just a little something". They weren't joking when they said a little something! 56p! Well, it got me ten fags.

I have lost count of the number of friends, here and in England, that are dead. The times I have got down on my knees to a pusher when I'd no money for a fix and was starting withdrawal, and screamed and screamed for a "hot shot".

Two years ago, I nearly made it. I was taken in

to the Adelaide in a coma. When I came to, I admitted to myself "I am a junkie" and said to the doctors "I'm a drug addict, help me". I had *never* been able to say those things before. I could never say "junkie", "addict", in relation to myself, though I knew I was one. I was kept in hospital seven and a half weeks, put on barbiturates, then physeptone, then valium, to lessen the withdrawals. Withdrawals get worse each time you get dried out. Shivering, shaking, cold and hot sweats, running nose, running eyes, fits, flashbacks, cravings, cramps, intense panic, sleeplessness, nightmares, intense agitation.

A couple of days after becoming drug-free, I went along to the drug-free therapeutic community in Coolemine Lodge. Now, to be fair, I didn't stay in Coolemine long enough to be able to pass judgement on the therapy there, and whether it is of any real long lasting value to the addict. But I did think afterwards that the comparison between the assessment of a person for Coolemine and Rutland was vast. The Rutland assessment is very thorough, and they will not accept a person if the programme will not suit that particular individual. The assessment for Coolemine, I thought, seemed to take the attitude that all addicts are much the same — what has worked for the two directors, founders of the place, and for various ex-residents of Coolemine, will work for you.

Physically I was fine when I went to Coolemine, but psychologically I was a wreck. And in my opinion there is not enough emphasis on assessing the psychology of the person going to Coolemine. It's a tough, tough programme. After a couple of weeks of trying to function, to live, to cope, to co-operate while every fibre in my body was screaming out as though I were on a bad acid trip, I was sure I was heading for a breakdown. I split from the place and a few days later did suffer a breakdown. The way I felt when I was there, and the subsequent breakdown, were not caused by Coolemine. I was just not psychologically strong enough at the time to take such an intense programme.

It was the first time I had genuinely wanted help to stay off drugs. I hadn't realised that I was in for such a shock. I didn't know it would be so difficult. It's not just a matter of getting dried out and trying one's hardest to stay off drugs. Your hardest is not enough, and eight times out of ten it's too late for "enough" anyway. Trying to stay drug-free is as horrifying and as mind-blowing as when you sink into the depths of addiction. The shock the mind and body take! The length of time it takes for both to get back to normal is unbelievable, and very frightening.

You are considered a failure if you do not complete the programme at Coolemine. Fair enough, if you split because you want nothing else except to get back into the scene again, or if you only give the place a week's trial and then decide it's not for you. But to consider a person a failure when they have tried their hardest, but, like me, are just not able for the intensity of the programme, is a terrible judgment.

There is a terrific tendency of the powers in charge of drug addicts — to typecast us. Just like the attitude of most of the public: "All drug addicts come from deprived backgrounds." "All university students are no-good drug addicts." "All drug addicts are immature emotionally." "All drug addicts have long hair, play the guitar, listen to heavy rock, are dirty, read Dylan Thomas, go on protest marches, go to pop festivals, and drawl 'cool it', 'crazy man', 'wow, dig it, like you know what I mean, man'."

To such people we are drug addicts first, individuals with personalities second. They group us all together and treat us all the same. I mean, we're not individuals, are we? Jack the junkie thinks such and such a way — well, then, so must Mary, Mark, Susan, Danny. "See that girl over there? She's a drug addict." Not, "That girl's name is Lisa." "Do you take drugs? Gosh! What's it like to be a drug addict?" "That guy's on drugs? How do you know?" "It's obvious, look at the cut of him, and the length of his hair!" Just like being under a microscope, being scrutinised. We are either a source of curiosity, a novelty, because we have the label "drug addict", "junkie", or we are to be scorned, shunned, talked down to as if we were moronic, blamed for anything that's out of the ordinary, unconventional in our society, treated like dirt.

There's no denying it, we are terribly tiresome and troublesome, and certainly don't command respect, but we *are* people, and we are people *first*. It's a frightful thing to typecast any person, to make an analysis of a person based on our own assumption, and more often than not incorrect assumption, of how so and so should behave and to treat them accordingly. It's a horrible feeling to be typecast, to feel you are a carbon copy of somebody's ludicrous and narrow-minded opinion.

I'm not saying the Coolemine directors took this kind of over-simplified view. But I didn't feel they made enough allowances for the individual character of each addict in the programme. Anyway, I had a complete mental breakdown and had to go into St. Patrick's. I went straight back on drugs when I was discharged. I started up my "junkie parlour" and "shooting gallery" again. So I was back into dealing in a pretty big way. I hated what I was doing, but it kept my habit going. I got busted again and was sent back to Brendan's. This time, I was put in a padded cell and did cold turkey. I took fits so bad that I ended up in the intensive care in the Mater. I lost the use of my leg and arm, and of my speech. My mouth was twisted in a grotesque fashion. I was like that for a week.

Again I went back on drugs. Got very heavily back into acid. I had to go into hospital for four months for operations on my feet and toes. I managed to get gear every three or four days. I also saved up the painkillers I was on. When I was able to get out of bed and get around in a wheelchair, I got syringes that had been discarded. I had brought in a couple of needles, but I managed to get a few in the hospital.

Then my contact stopped coming in as I owed far too much money. Of course, my supply ran out and I started withdrawals. At this time I was using liquid methedrine, dyke and popping as much valium as I could get. I tried discharging myself, but I wasn't even able to use the crutches yet. I was in a frightful state of panic, so I got the doctor on duty and told him I was having a breakdown and that it seemed to be taking the form of severe withdrawals. They put me on Heminevrin. By the end of February I was dropping twenty Heminevrin a day. I had seven prescriptions for them, all from different doctors. By March I had worked my way up to sixty a day. I was also taking about thirty to forty valium a day. I stopped taking anything else from February to June. Just heminevrin, heminevrin, heminevrin. I even tried fixing with them.

One day I read an article on Rutland. I jotted down the number and a week later rang them. I had an interview with one of the Counsellors who made an appointment for me in Jervis Street. I attended there as an outpatient every day for a month. I refused to come in as an inpatient. For the first two weeks I did very well, then I started using dyke again and getting scripts for heminevrin as well as being given heminevrin in the clinic. In desperation I allowed the psychiatrist to admit me.

I spent two months in the detoxification ward. It was hard. *Very* hard, but not as hard as trying to stay drug free. It's taking determination, patience and courage. I still have all the problems that I used to shut out by drugs.

When you have dried out completely you think your problems will disappear just like that! Hah! Like hell they do. Sure you have a serious, deadly problem while taking drugs, but the shock when you come out of the haze of drugs is mind-blowing.

Most addicts are emotionally fourteen or fifteen-years old, even though they might be twenty-four or twenty-six or even thirty. Facing up to reality, everyday tensions, stress, strain, doing tasks which are a cinch for most people, taking responsibilities — and I don't mean big responsibilities — making decisions, discovering your true self and personality, trying to cope with different emotions that are totally alien as they were suppressed by drugs throughout the teenage years — all this is very difficult. Growing. Maturing. None of those problems arose when on drugs — how could they? So to anyone who thinks: "Well, she's off drugs now, we can breathe a long sigh of relief and relax; no more problems", I say: "Hold in that sigh of relief for at least two years, then let it out and relax." Because it can take two to three years before the psychological problems are sorted out.

* * *

The government makes me sick. They put millions

of pounds into building roads. They're putting millions into building an airport at Knock that in all honesty we don't need. And there are girls and boys of eight, nine, ten, eleven, twelve, thirteen and fourteen sniffing glue and sniffing it openly. There are ten, eleven, twelve and thirteen-year-old children hooked on heroin.

In God's name, we have a major drug crisis on our hands and it's spreading rapidly around Ireland. We are on the same scale as New York. People are being murdered for money for drugs — bank raids, post office raids, mugging. Why the *hell* doesn't the government put money into building at least three detoxification units for these kids, and not a unit with just nine beds, like Jervis Street. *And* why don't they buy two more houses and have a programme like Coolemine for the youngsters who are dried out. Jervis Street can't cope with the ever-growing number of drug addicts.

As for justice — the judges! Are they living in cloud cuckoo land? Known drug dealers can get three-month sentences — people who have got young kids hooked on drugs, people with blood on their hands! And it's not just that dealing in hard drugs is dealing in death. These people deal in wholesale violence, too. Clients who can't pay, or who threaten to talk, get beaten up by their suppliers. Terrorist tactics are used to keep you in line.

I have been beaten up four times since I was seventeen. I could never tell the doctors what really happened. I was far too frightened. On one occasion, I had my back kicked brutally. Two girls and two guys kicked me to the ground and kept kicking me in the small of my back with their shoes and smashing it with their fists. I got a slipped disc as a result and eventually had to have it removed as no amount of physiotherapy could get it back into place. I told everyone I fell down the stairs so as to explain away all the bruises.

The first time I was done over, I was brought to a flat and beaten across the face. I had my hair cut all jagged and I was kicked in the stomach — then driven back to where they had picked me up. I stayed with friends until the bruises on my face had gone. No addict is going to tell the police or the drug squad who beats them up. No addict would go to court to give evidence — you'd be signing your death warrant.

Another time, three girls burst into my bedsitter, beat me around the head and scratched my face and neck with their nails. And another time I was pounced on by three girls and five boys who knocked me senseless and then dumped me outside the casualty ward of a hospital. Decent of them! I had concussion for three days.

It's not just open violence, either. If you look as if you're escaping, they try to drag you back to drugs, even if they have to give you free gear for a while so as to keep you as a "good customer".

There's one gang in particular who, even now, remind me now and then that there's no way I'm

going to make it. About three months ago I was
going to a friend's house. I had to pass a pub that's
well known for dope fiends. Two guys came out of
the pub as I was passing by. They were two out of
the gang that hassle the hard drug addict. They
started jeering at me over the fact that I was
straight, dry. Then they actually blocked my way
and, oh God, held out a handful of pills, told me I
could have them for nothing. I kicked one of them
on the leg and ran, and didn't stop running until I
was back in my flat. Oh, how I wanted those pills
the minute I saw them!

Some junkies and dealers will hassle you until
they wear you down and you just say "oh, shit, I
might as well", and then — finito. You're right
back to where you started. There's a lot of resentment and hatred among some addicts towards
addicts that have gone straight and are trying to
stay that way.

Chapter 22

Operation Appendix

When I was on hard drugs, I used to do amazing things just to get into hospital to obtain drugs. The most incredible incident — incredible in its outcome — was when I decided to "develop" appendicitis so that I could get painkillers for nothing after the operation — if everything went according to plan. On the evening I put my plan into operation (horrible pun!), I convinced myself that I felt a slight pain in my abdomen — oh so *very* slight! I knew that a friend would be coming over later, and I wanted to convince her that it wasn't just a bad stomach upset but something far more serious. When she knocked on the door of my bedsitter, I opened the door, clutching my stomach and saying in a strained, strangled voice: "Look, get me to a hospital. I've had this pain for two days and it's getting worse." I staggered over to the bed and lay down, groaning very effectively.

My friend rang for an ambulance immediately, and I moaned and groaned all the way to a certain large Dublin hospital. She came along with me. I was rushed into the hospital on a stretcher and a doctor examined me at once. My temperature, pulse and blood pressure were all normal. I knew more or less — well, rather more than less — where the appendix was located, so when the doctor pressed my right side, I cried out in agony and begged him not to do it again. "Oh, oh God, the pain is getting worse. I think I'm going to pass out, doctor."

Eventually he went away and my friend came into the cubicle. She told me that one of the nurses had asked her for my name, address and age — that was all right — and also about any past illnesses I had had. Well, my friend knew quite a lot about me, and to my horror and rage the first thing she had told them was that I was a drug addict! She had to do it, I know, but that part of hospital procedure had never entered my head beforehand. Still, even drug addicts are entitled to have appendicitis!

At 11.30 I was wheeled up to a ward, put into bed and examined again. I was getting a bit fed up at this stage; I was also very tired and just wanted to go asleep. I was worried in case I would forget and say "ouch", "oh" or "oh God" if he pressed any other part of my stomach. But he just pressed the right side and I kept up my moans and groans and ouches. Soon after midnight, he told me he was putting me on a drip and that I would be going down to theatre in about an hour. Up went the drip, and out came the razor blade and I was dutifully shaved. Then, at about two in the morning, I was brought to the theatre. I was woken up in the recovery room and the first thing I asked was the time. One of the nurses told me it was just after four. I remember thinking hazily how odd that was, since an appendix operation is supposed to be quick, so it should be about three o'clock now.

I fell back asleep again. When I woke up it was morning, and I was vomiting and in genuine pain. As the day went on, the pain didn't cease — after all, I *had* been opened up and cut with a knife. I was given no pain-killing injection, no tablets — nothing! Then the white coats and stethoscopes arrived. Before they asked me how I was feeling, I said: "Look, can you give me something for the pain, please?" The house surgeon replied: "No Lisa, we can't give you anything on account of your addiction. I'm really sorry. I know how sore you are, but we can't give you anything."

Then a tall, grey-haired doctor said, "You're a lucky girl — very lucky." He proceeded to tell me the incredible outcome of my so-called appendicitis. Apparently when the house surgeon opened me up, he couldn't find the appendix. He rooted around but still couldn't find it. So they had to call in a senior surgeon, who found the appendix behind the bowel. The next thing he said nearly sent me into a state of shock. He told me my appendix was highly inflamed and would have perforated if it had been left a few days longer. I will never understand how I had no real pain if that was the case. The very slight pain I felt when I willed myself to have a pain was purely my imagination — I'm sure of that.

Well, I had no intention of staying in hospital if I wasn't going to get any pain-killers, so when they took the drip off the next morning, I got my clothes out of the locker. When the ambulance men had brought me in the day before, I had been wearing no coat or shoes, only slippers. There were four other patients in the ward, but they didn't take any notice of what I was doing. I told one of them I had been discharged as it was only a minor operation. The nurses' station was at the other end of the corridor and there were no nurses anywhere near the ward at that time. I borrowed a sheet of paper, an envelope and a pen from one of the patients and wrote a note saying I was discharging myself. Then I put it in the envelope, wrote "staff nurse" on the outside, and left it on top of the locker. I hid my clothes under my dressing-gown and went into the bathroom to get dressed. I stuffed my nightdress and dressing-gown into my hold-all. There were two ways of getting down the stairs to freedom. One was to the left, past the nurses' station, the other to the right, past an operating theatre and on down towards the stairs. So I turned to the right. I'll never forget it. I kept telling myself: "Don't dare faint. Just keep on walking down the stairs." Eventually I made my way to the waiting room, where I asked a porter if I could ring for a taxi. At last I was back in my bedsitter.

I was afraid to go back to the hospital to get my stitches out a week later so I took them out myself. I must have made a good job of it. I swore I would never go into a hospital on any sort of pretext again — I had been shocked by what the surgeon told me and by the fact that I couldn't get even an aspirin. I've been through a lot of operations and illnesses since then, but they have all been authentic. But — I'll say it again — I had no real pain that time I was rushed to that hospital and got my appendix out. That's the truth.

Chapter 23

The World of Drugs

The world of drugs has been rightly called a lonely world of mental frustration, false happiness, and sickness. You enter it so simply, for kicks, for an escape from your problems or from yourself. Drugs are attractive because they promise the kind of happiness for which people have always been willing to risk the gravest dangers. But this is only a false happiness. Real well-being can only be reached by personal effort and toil.

I want to say something about the effects of some of the best known drugs. Hash, for instance, is the most widely used. For teenagers, it is a great way of defying middle-aged beliefs. It's "cool" because it's illegal, yet it isn't supposed to be habit-forming.

But that is *not* true! OK, I'm not saying that if you smoke a joint you are going to get hooked on heroin. But because cannabis disturbs your mind and your judgment, you can easily be led into harder drugs. Hash gives you the drug sensation, it opens the door, and makes you unwary enough to step through that door into the world of drugs.

LSD is a trip into total insanity. Recurrence of a bad trip can happen without warning, and is terribly frightening. And for women taking LSD, their children may be born with brain damage or physically deformed.

Amphetamines cause abnormal heart rhythms, and can even lead to permanent brain damage. Users are prone to malnutrition, pneumonia and mental and physical exhaustion because they go without food and sleep for long periods. I know this is true, in my case, because I went down to seven stone, and nearly died from a dangerous ailment of my digestive system which, they told me, usually occurs in middle-aged alcoholic men!

With cocaine, the user is prone to frightful depression, dizziness and mental confusion, and may attack people either verbally or physically. Usually, it's a physical attack on people who they think are out to "get them", or trying to "get at them over the slightest thing". Or they think that everybody is talking about them. I don't know why I'm saying "they" — that was exactly the way my *own* behaviour was. And withdrawals from cocaine are absolutely agonising.

Heavy doses of barbiturates cause depression and total apathy. After taking a big dose of barbs, you go into a deep sleep or even coma. Physical co-ordination goes haywire — you act like a dead drunk person. You tend to have accidents, and you don't feel the pain at the time. You forget how many barbs you have taken, so you can easily take an accidental overdose. If you take them with alcohol you can go straight into coma and quite possibly die. Once I mixed barbs with wine and only by the grace of God did I come out of the coma. The doctors gave me a couple of hours to live, and told my parents there was nothing they could do — I was in God's hands now.

Morphine attacked my mind and self-control. I quickly became a mental degenerate. Also, I took convulsions five times, four times while in St. Brendan's for the "cure". Withdrawal from morphine is extremely painful and highly dangerous. Chills, sweating, runny nose, watery eyes, and frightful agitation.

I'm sorry I can't paint a more romantic picture of drug addiction. But that's the way it is. It's disgusting.

If you could have seen me when I was a really bad junkie! I was covered in boils and sores. There was a big abscess on my arms, my teeth were rotten. I'd gone down to seven stone, I was filthy, my language was foul, my talk was junkie street talk, I wore the same clothes for months, I never washed, my face had caved in, I used to sleep for about an hour now and then, then I was off speeding around again, sleeping rough, eating out of dustbins. I was a mental and physical wreck. I have lost so much of my life. Years have gone by that I don't remember anything about. I've wasted my teenage years, and I got into a life of crime — all to keep my habit going.

A junkie's "life" is an existence, a self delusion involving crime, lies, filth, using people for one's own means. It is immaturity, vicious, violent, irresponsible, abnormal, without conscience or proper emotions or feelings, except for negative and destructive ones. It is a life of degradation, of squalor, of being at death's door, of aggressiveness. After a couple of years there is a feeling of inferiority, lack of confidence, no respect for oneself, a frightful sense of loneliness even in a crowd. It is life lived in a kind of "limbo". But there is still a *desperate* need to be loved, wanted, a sort of crying out to be needed and cared about.

Chapter 24

Another Setback

Staying off drugs is a terrible strain. One thing I can't take is people's lack of understanding — the majority of people — that the addict goes through *sheer hell* after kicking the habit. I tell people "look, I really have far more problems now than I ever did when I was on gear." But they won't believe me.

The worst thing an addict can face is the look of disgust, the cold shoulder, the attitude of "oh, I give up, after all we did for her", as if we had committed an unforgiveable crime.

Nearly every junkie has a setback, a relapse, even if they have been off drugs for several years. There's no good being ashamed of it, you simply have to keep on trying. But Jesus! — the awful need in the pit of your stomach to be wanted, the awful, bitchy facade you show to the world because you don't want to be made a fool of. Even when people put up with you, it's hard to believe they really like you.

Not that we're always easy to like. They say addicts are smart manipulators. How I hate that word! We use a great deal of cleverness to blackmail, we use every weapon from threats to violence. We can't tell the truth, even when we're confronted with the truth, like a person saying "yes, you *did* take something, look at you, you're stoned out of your mind!" But half the time we genuinely believe we *haven't* taken anything. One thing though, in my case: I greatly respect and admire people who are able to hold out against me. I'm talking now in the present tense, because I did have a setback, even since starting to write this book. I lied. Crucified myself. Refused to mix. Tried suicide once. I was so full of guilt and shame — but I'm back on that long, long road again, towards a normal drug-free life. I can't say if I will make it. But the very *worst* thing to do, actually, is to give in to shame, self-disgust, revulsion and guilt, because that's only prolonging the misery. You feel like such a social leper and it's an easy excuse for keeping on going downhill to the gutter I once was in, and to run away from facing reality again. Even a short setback can be an excuse to wallow in self-pity and go back on drugs permanently.

I made out a list one day of all the drugs I had been addicted to. It was a long list: codeine, veganin, tuinal, seconal, nembutal, sodium amytal, mandrax, luminal, valium, diconal, palfium, pondrax, ionamin, benzedrine, pethidine, dexedrine, morphine, antihistamines, heminevrin, ritalin ... And the drugs I've dabbled in: cocaine, acid, mescalin. I snorted smack (heroin) for two weeks. But I never mainlined it.

That was when I decided I was coming off the hard drugs. I went back home and I was really strung out. Sick. I tried cold turkey and stuck it out only three days and gave in. I had been snorting smack for about a fortnight — how I never mainlined it is beyond me. I just stayed in bed, sniffing heroin, popping barbs and — of all things! — antihistamine pills. After a few days I began to feel that something awfully serious was happening to me, that part of my brain had stopped functioning. I climbed out of bed and found I was unable to walk. I couldn't feel my legs or arms. There was just no feeling. And I had cigarette burns on my fingers and hands.

My parents brought me in to the Adelaide — I owe an awful lot to that hospital, it's one place I really trust. I wasn't capable of walking or talking properly for about a week. The physician and the psychiatrist decided against sending me to a psychiatric hospital. They dried me out for seven and a half weeks in the Adelaide, and all I received from the doctors, the nurses, the matron, assistant matron, the night sisters, and the other patients, was pure kindness and understanding. At the end of that time a girl and boy from the Coolemine community came in to talk to me. They came back to see me again, and the third time they called I made my mind up to go to Coolemine. So the following week, when I was completely dry of medication, I was collected by the co-director of Coolemine and one of the girls on the staff who had come to visit me.

But I didn't make it at Coolemine. I've already written about why I think the set-up didn't suit me and my problems. Today, when I have changed and Coolemine has changed, things might work out differently.

Have you ever spent a night out in the rain? I've spent days and nights walking in the rain, soaked to the skin with the rain and my own sweat. I did that for five days and nights once. I had a bedsitter to go to at the time, but I just wanted to keep walking to try and get my head together. I was trying to come off barbs and speed by myself. Drenched with rain and perspiration, I don't know which was wetting me most, the cold water or the sweat. Well, I didn't get off the barbs or the speed that time, but I did get an attack of pleurisy, and I was stuck in bed for ten weeks. Another setback.

Coming off drugs can be a terrifying experience. The two serious convulsions I took last year were a result of bringing myself down from an incredible dose of Heminevrin over a period of ten days. I still don't know what made my mind go completely haywire for over a week after I had recovered from the second convulsion.

The tension fits are different. Those are the fits I take when all my muscles stiffen up and my jaw locks. That comes from high-pitched anxiety and tension, not from withdrawals — it can't be withdrawals, because it happens when I haven't been anywhere near drugs. But I know they will stop in the end, because at long last I have told two doctors about some of my complexes and how they came about, and actually I really did feel relaxed and free once that dam burst open that I had kept closed up to myself since the age of thirteen. Even under LSD treatment and abreaction and gestalt therapy and group therapy I didn't talk about it. But now I can come out slowly with all the heartbreak, all the reasons why I was a sure-fire candidate for hard-core drug addiction, the misery of my life from when I was thirteen right up to the time I broke down that barrier, that dam of emotions and misery — can it be only a few weeks ago? But I'm not going to write about my real feelings all those years. I've started to talk about them, to my doctors, to my mother, and at the beginning of this book I gave some hint of the hell I lived in inside my head while I was still at school. I find it exhausting to talk about that hell now — relaxing but exhausting. My head clears, but my eyes turn into two swollen red saucers in my face.

Until I finally clear the dirt inside my head over the things I did to get money for drugs, I will never be a whole person, only a half human being. I've got to get it into my head that all that is in the past now, and that I'm as good as anyone else — but I've still got a king-size chip on my shoulder. Of course it's also an excuse for my failures, my faults and so on: "oh, well, I've been on drugs for ten and a half years, so what can you expect?" Wow, what a cop-out! Using my years of addiction as an excuse for my behaviour today ... Lisa, sometimes you make me sick!

One thing that does *not* help is the belief that people have that drugs can be cured through a simple act of faith. Three years ago, I got into reading books by the Rev. David Wilkinson, books like *The Cross and the Switchblade*. OK, he has a great story to tell, how he started his crusade with a friend by going into places at night where even teams of cops wouldn't dare to go, preaching to gangs of addicts who carried flick-knives and murdered for the sake of murdering. So he started preaching and calling on the Lord to help these poor, lost souls — *not* that I'm knocking God, definitely not! Anyway, these wild-eyed, flick-knived heroin addicts went down on their knees, weeping and repenting. They threw away their knives and were cured of their addiction, through listening to the sermons of the Rev. David Wilkinson. (I think Pat Boone starred in the film).

But it isn't really as simple as that. Addicts have to be withdrawn slowly. They can die if they're not given medication to substitute the drug they're on, and detoxified for weeks. Then, there's eighteen months in a therapeutic community like Coolemine (if they don't split), before they are fully cured.

Conversion and faith are not enough. Sure, pray to God for strength, but don't think you can free yourself from drugs just by being converted and making an act of faith. I will probably have half the population of Ireland down on top of me for saying this, but I don't care. In my opinion, for somebody thinking about trying to get off drugs, these books are positively dangerous. They promise too much hope.

In all my years of addiction, one of the most horrific things I had to do was one night when two friends and myself were just setting out for a walk, and we came on another friend of ours, a heroin addict. She was lying outside her flat, clutching her stomach, shaking all over, sweating profusely, rambling in her speech. There was a syringe beside her, and in her bag the works for cooking up the heroin, but she was shaking all over because she had been trying to kick the habit and was going through frightful withdrawals. She had only got the H an hour before we came on her, and she was in such a state that she was totally incapable of shooting it into a vein. She had been popping valium by the bottle. We carried her into her pad. In between the ramblings, she kept begging us to cook up the H for her and shoot it into her ourselves. So we got the powder onto a spoon, mixed it with water and heated it up. Two of us held her down and kept her arm steady, while another found a vein for the needle. But then she started to jerk, and gasp, and turn a ghastly colour. Then she went unconscious. We had given her too big a dose by accident. So we called an ambulance. One of my friends was giving her mouth-to-mouth resuscitation. At last the ambulance came and they took her away to hospital. We weren't allowed to come with her. But we did manage to get in touch with her family. She was in the intensive care unit for three days, in a coma. When she came out of the coma, they moved her to Jervis Street. Later, she moved on to Coolemine, stayed for (I think) four months and then split. Back onto the street. Back shooting smack. And a year and a half later she was found by her brother in her bedroom, dead.

Accidental? Deliberate? No-one will ever know. She was a lovely girl. Beautiful looking, and a beautiful person. She really, really wanted to make it.

Do you know how she started on drugs? One night, when she was in a pub, enjoying a folk session, a "friend" spiked her drink. It was done for a joke. But the joke turned into a nightmare for her. She went on a fantastic high that night, and being no fool she guessed what had happened. She left the pub with tabs in her pocket, and information about where to get more, about the prices of gear, and so on. She was so intelligent. She knew what would happen. She used to tell me to kick the habit, that I would die before I ever saw eighteen.

I've tried all kinds of ways to get off drugs. Reading books on Zen, studying books and pamphlets on self-help, going to the Christian Science people, to Recovery, to the Inner Peace movement, doing gestalt workouts on my own, attending prayer meetings for four months. What did all this do for me? No comment! One thing that was a great help, though, was the Assertiveness Training that I did with a social worker in hospital once. That certainly enabled me to get my life back into some sort of order.

I wasn't always accepted by the people I turned to for help. When I came out of Jervis Street while trying to get off Heminevrin, I tried to get outpatient treatment in a centre where young addicts come in every day to do woodwork and pottery. I thought this would help me a lot, but the doctor in charge told me that because of my past history of hard drug abuse they couldn't take me in. I was too "sophisticated" an addict, and it simply wouldn't be fair on the newer addicts there, who hadn't reached my stage — as yet.

Then I went on acupuncture. And that's when I cut down from 92 caps a day to only one, within a month and a half of treatment. It really did help a lot with that frightful tension and anxiety, but I think the fact that I got down to one a day, and then none a day, was basically "mind over matter" — because when the acupuncturist went on his holidays, the anxiety and tension started getting bad again even though I had the little pins in. And one weekend, when he was back in town but off duty, I took four tension fits one after the other. The usual. Muscles stiffening up, jaw locking. A friend stayed with me right through the weekend, and three doctors had to come out — but their anxiety was more acute than mine because I was unable to pay them!

I must have had a psychological dependency on that acupuncturist, because when he wasn't there to stick pins in me and reassure me, look what happened.

Over a period of months before writing these pages, I have gone through the most incredible emotional turmoil. Frightful stress, strain, terrible unhappiness. None of this was related to drug abuse, because I have been on supervised medication — nothing addictive. But I have a great GP now, one of the best, most broadminded, no-nonsense, kindest people, who doesn't pull his punches, makes me face reality, accepts no excuses or rationalisations for my behaviour. He hates having to give me any medication at all, but it is very necessary.

I'm not going to go into the past few months, and what went wrong for me, and why everything went wrong. But my whole world fell down on top of me, and I very nearly didn't come out from underneath the rubble. One day, I swallowed a packet of darning needles, a box of nails, and some open safety pins. Part of me desperately wanted to die, part of me wanted help. One of the darning needles got stuck in my throat. So I rang my doctor. That was the part of me that wanted help. I was rushed into hospital in the middle of the night. They brought me down to the theatre at three o'clock in the morning. Part of the needle was nearly perforating the wall of my gullet, and although I don't understand the medical jargon the doctors used after the operation when they explained how the needle was lodged, I know they had quite a job getting it out. I want to thank the staff of that hospital, who were so kind and understanding and anxious to help. I started facing up honestly to reality and myself again, just in a small way — but it was a start.

Then, when I was back in my flat, the strain I was under got worse and became totally unbearable again, and my mind felt as if it had been blown open. I don't know if I had been going through a breakdown, but anyway, at 2 a.m. one night my head exploded and I got the carving knife and smashed a glass and slashed and slashed and slashed into my arms, then flung away the knife and the piece of glass and ran to the phone and rang the Samaritans screaming for help. Two volunteers came over at once and brought me in to Jervis Street. The doctors there stitched me up, but because I had lost so much blood, they refused to let me go home again with the two volunteers, who had stayed on waiting for me. I was determined to get back to my flat, but gave in finally because I was feeling so awful.

Two weekends later, back in the flat, I overdosed. I didn't know I was going to overdose. The thought was certainly not in my mind. I remember getting on a bus, early on the Saturday. Then I remember waking up, undressed — just in my nightdress — on the floor of my living-room in the flat, surrounded by empty medicine bottles. Four empty bottles, all of different kinds of tablets, different types of tranquillisers. These tabs can only be got on scripts, but I had no prescription. It was three o'clock in the afternoon — Monday afternoon. That frightened me — oh, I can't express *how* it frightened me.

I have my own ideas about what should have been done for me when I was first taken into hospital with convulsions, instead of discharging me while I was still hallucinating and jerking and raving like an idiot. But I won't go into blaming doctors and hospitals here. Anyway, I did come up from underneath the rubble, and I think I came up a stronger person.

Just because of what I said earlier in this book against Coolemine (and I want to emphasise that Coolemine has got better since I was there), I don't want people to think I gave up drugs on my own. My flatmates, and the girls next door, made a sort of "Coolemine" in my life for me. I was confronted with my behaviour, forced to face home truths and take decisions. When I behaved like a spoiled brat, they treated me like one. I was made aware of how much I lied about taking drugs, even when I was screaming and shouting that I hadn't taken anything at all, because I was ashamed of letting down people who really cared, or because I couldn't remember, or because I just didn't want to admit the truth. They put me through a lot. They let me know exactly what I was like under the influence of drugs. But thank God for friends like those. They made life very hard for me, but if they hadn't done that, God knows what I'd be now. I didn't get pity from them, but I did get comfort and support when I needed it. I love them. I'm glad they gave me hell. But it *was* hard! They used to say: "You're only fooling yourself, you're certainly not fooling us" — and they were right. I was so lucky (horrible word!) to have those girls for friends. Friends like that are rare, and they certainly gave me some "rare old times".

What I'd like to write on this page is "Here endeth the saga of the true life of a junkie" — but I know the struggle is far from over. I'm not safe yet, never will be safe. Slowly, very slowly, I'm building up my life and getting myself together. The one thing in my favour is that I'm a fighter. I always bounce back again when I've been beaten down and trodden underfoot. A fighter for survival is what I've always been, and that's what I'll always fight for. Survival.

Epilogue

Dear Mammy and Dad,

I want to tell you how much I love you both — but I can't. I start feeling too inhibited when I pluck up the courage to say "I love you both". *Ridiculous* embarrassment on my part!

I'm deeply, deeply sorry for the hurt, the misery, the turmoil, the anguish, the desperation that I put you through over the years. Well, it's over now. I can't say, in all honesty, if I will stay off drugs for good. No "dry" addict can say that. But I will keep trying, fighting every day to stay off them — as I'm doing now. One thing in my favour, though. I have an absolute abhorrence towards drugs. I'm becoming very strong, and very determined, and I intend to stay that way.

What wonderful parents you are! You stuck by me all those years. Never giving up hope. How you must love me. When the doctors in Jervis Street told you, eighteen months ago, that there was no real hope for me, nothing more they could do for me, *you* didn't stop hoping. As you said, "parents should never give up, they must keep giving their children a chance." It could be that one last chance that could work, you said.

In my case, I had tried so hard, and so many times, to come off drugs, and it *was* that one last chance which worked for me.

I really appreciate your acceptance of the way I

was. That, I know, was by no means easy. The love you gave me. I know how difficult everything was for you. To have somebody who was a wayward, troublesome, hateful bitch, who nearly wrecked your lives, who nearly wrecked your emotions by exhausting them to breaking point.

Maybe some day you will read this. In the meantime, I can show my love for you in little ways, little ways that have been and still are a big effort for me, but an effort which I have managed for the past few months, and which I'm determined to keep up, especially the hard, hard battle to stay off drugs.

I want you to be proud of me.
I love you both.
"Lisa"

Afterword
by Dr. Tony Peacock

When asked some weeks ago to write my thoughts
on this book, I considered what lay ahead of me to
be a daunting task, to say the least. For the past
year I have been involved to some extent in the
rehabilitation of Lisa, and knowing her as well as I
do, I am aware of the immense complexity of her
personality. While the literary merits of this book
may be judged by people better qualified than I, it
is fair to say that the contents of the preceding
pages represent only a fraction of the experiences
she has related to me in consultation. I am also
limited in my direct knowledge of her, as I have
only had experience of just one year of her life, at
a time when she was beginning to make some sort
of therapeutic progress. Much has gone before
which I do not have eye-witness evidence of.

What strikes me personally about Lisa is a totally

186

uninhibited manifestation of the broad spectrum
of human emotions; her personality is as complex
— if not more so — as that of other members of the
human race, but her expression of anger, fear, joy,
etc. is more direct and less apologetic than social
mores generally allow. Her innocence is all-
pervading. It may have been on account of this
childlike innocence that she was lured into these
horrific experiences. However this is a personal
impression and this quality should in no way be
taken as the sole cause of her downfall. In saying
the word "downfall", it must be earnestly hoped
that her fight for recovery will be successful and
that her recent predicaments will not recur. She
has also shown a resilience which is rare in "many a
tougher breed". Up to this time, she has at least
attempted to pick up the pieces of her shattered
life, to allow herself some form of cohesive personal
identity, and from that, independence. It would be
unfair to say that she has not had set-backs, but
her will to get up and fight again puts her in the
ranks of the minority.

On a more general note, it must be stressed that
for every person like Lisa who wins the battle,
there are many more who lose it and this is the
fearsome prospect for anyone contemplating a
"career" such as Lisa's. Having read the book a
number of times, I began to realise how complacent
society is with regard to this problem. I have
spoken to many people who are firmly convinced
that the problem is confined virtually exclusively

to the so-called "lower classes". This is not so, as my own experience and that of other general practitioners will testify. It is all too easy for those of us who have a certain degree of security — in as far as times will allow — to sit back with not only a degree of distance but also a measure of aloofness from this ever-increasing problem of drug addiction. I feel also that the experiences related by Lisa reflect only a small portion of the full picture of drug addiction in Ireland today.

Since we hear most about addictions to heroin, LSD and such drugs — which represent the most dramatic cases and therefore reach the media — we tend to be somewhat unaware of other addictions, especially to substances like "simple" pain-killers, minor tranquillisers, sleeping tablets and cough mixtures. The fact is that over the past twenty years or so we have become an extremely drug-orientated society, holding the false belief that drugs for the most part are the cure for all ills. This tends to be the case more especially in mental illness, where the commonest agents prescribed are minor tranquillisers. Many people are still under the impression that recovery is possible only with the aid of drugs such as these. However, there is a slow but sure move towards a situation where patients are becoming less reliant on drugs as the "cure-all" and are directed instead to treatments such as psychotherapy and various forms of relaxation programmes.

In all fairness to the pharmaceutical industry, it

should be stressed that not all drug therapy is bad. An extreme of no drugs for anything is as wrong as the extreme of only drugs for everything. The solution lies in maintaining a policy whereby drugs are prescribed only where necessary and blind trials of drugs for unspecific symptoms are firmly avoided. The solution to the problem of drug abuse and excessive prescribing of drugs lies also in bringing doctors and patients to an awareness of the fact that natural recovery can only be achieved by the use of some drugs, which are properly and accurately prescribed. Many drugs prescribed today treat the symptoms but not the cause. We have all to some extent begun to rely on drugs as the sole cure for all ills. Walk into your local pharmacy and see the shelves stocked full of drugs which purport to cure everything, from "neurasthenia" and "debility" to the "common cold". All of these are readily available without prescription. Many of these preparations can result in harmful side-effects if not taken in correct dosage. This is especially true of vitamin preparations.

Lisa herself is a product of a society which is dependent on drugs, except that her case is more extreme than the average. We can all reflect on ourselves and ask how many times have we regularly taken bottles of "tonics", spoonfuls of cough mixture, jars of vitamins, or packets of pain-killers for the slightest headache. We all exhibit the minor symptoms of a major social illness and none of us can point a finger at the "hard" drug abuser without at least recognising the fact that most of us bear some guilt.

The situation can only radically change if a sincere, concerted effort is made by the medical and pharmaceutical professions to do all in their power to ensure that what drugs we have are used in a responsible manner, and also to foster the idea that drugs alone are not the answer to many of society's ills. Then hopefully there will not be too many more Lisas frequenting the streets and detoxification units.

T. Peacock MB

Another Ward River Bestseller!

PAPERFACTS 7

DRUGS
and
young people

James Comberton

guaranteed
irish

"My child would never take drugs"

"Ireland has no drug problem"

These attitudes are sadly out of date. Every day in
this country more young people experiment with
drugs, and are gradually drawn into dependence.
For some, hooked on hard drugs, the future holds a
nightmare of crime, sickness and early death.
In most cases, their parents are completely
unaware of what is happening until it is too late.

James Comberton, Executive Chairman of
Coolmine Therapeutic Community, puts the whole
problem in perspective. He offers hard facts, calm
advice, and a practical guide to the very simple ways
in which you can help to safeguard your young
people's health and happiness.

PAPERFACTS 7

DRUGS
and
young people

James Comberton

guaranteed irish